In Memory of
Annie Edwards

In Honor of
Janice D. Stanton

Donated by
Elise H. Stephens

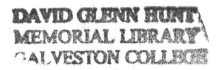

slavery:
its origin
and legacy

slavery: its origin and legacy

EDITED BY JOHN B. DUFF
AND LARRY A. GREENE
Seton Hall University

problem studies in american history

Thomas Y. Crowell Company

New York

Established 1834

The frontispiece is a magazine illustration reprinted by permission of the Schomburg Center for Research in Black Culture, The New York Public Library.

Library of Congress Cataloging in Publication Data

DUFF, JOHN B., comp.
  Slavery, its origin and legacy.

  (Problem studies in American history)
  Bibliography: p.
    1.   Slavery in the United States—History—Addresses,
essays, lectures.   2.   Slavery in Latin America—
History—Addresses, essays, lectures.   I.   Greene,
Larry, joint comp.   II.   Title.
III.   Series.
E441.D82   301.44'93'0973   74-22308
ISBN 0-690-00458-3

TO OUR FAMILIES

preface

Slavery has been called a historiographical perennial. From the time the first slaves arrived in Virginia in 1618 to our own day, Americans have argued over the nature of the slave system in the United States. Until the Emancipation Proclamation and the Thirteenth Amendment, slavery, of course, was a vital issue in American politics. Since then, it has become primarily a point of dispute among historians; but each generation has examined slavery in the context of the social, political and economic characteristics of the times.

James Ford Rhodes, the first accomplished historian to produce a scholarly study of slavery, found it to be an institution condemned by ethics, Christianity and science, as well as the primary cause of the Civil War. There have been several subsequent historiographical landmarks; in particular, U. B. Phillips's American Negro Slavery published in 1918; Kenneth Stampp's The Peculiar Institution (1956); Stanley Elkins's Slavery (1959); and in this decade Eugene D. Genovese's profound and monumental study, Roll, Jordan, Roll: The World the Slaves Made (1974) as well as Time on the Cross (1974) by Robert W. Fogel and Stanley L. Engerman, a book that some critics have described as destined to influence the writing of American history to the same extent as Frederick Jackson Turner's essays on the frontier and Charles A. Beard's An Economic Interpretation of the Constitution of the United States.

This collection of essays presents a broad sampling of what historians have said about slavery in the past century. In most cases, the readers will find these scholars to be in sharp disagreement with each other. It is, therefore, the task of the individual reader to judge for himself which historian makes the most persuasive case. Hopefully, these selections will encourage the reader to probe deeper into this controversial subject. For that reason, the editors have tried to include in the bibliography the most important and perceptive monographs and essays on the subject.

The editors wish to express their thanks to their colleagues in the department of history at Seton Hall University, particularly Peter M. Mitchell, for their interest and assistance in this project. Their deepest appreciation goes to Mrs. Ana Alves Russo who typed and proofread the entire manuscript.

John B. Duff

Larry A. Greene

contents

x

slavery:
its origin
and legacy

introduction

The Civil War and the Thirteenth Amendment abolished the
institution of slavery, but the controversy over the South's
"peculiar institution" which began long before the war has
continued until our own time. With each change in the Zeitgeist
affecting interpretations there is no reason to doubt that different
facets will be illuminated. Presently the debate over slavery
centers around several themes: the causal relationship between
the origins of slavery and of racial prejudice; the extent of slave
suffering; the creation of a childlike slave personality; the slave's
response to bondage; comparison with Latin American slavery;
and whether slavery could have been eliminated without civil
war.

Within each of these themes there are sociological, economic,
psychological, and political factors. One of the two major schools
of thought emphasizes the paternalistic nature of slavery, slave
docility, slave contentment, and the unprofitableness of a system
which would necessitate abolition rather than the need for war.
The other school emphasizes the oppressive character of slavery,
slave rebelliousness, and the profitability of an institution
making peaceful abolition improbable and unrealistic.

Which came first, slavery or prejudice, is the theme of the first
section dealing with origins. Since laws defining Negro slavery
in Virginia and Maryland did not appear until the 1660s,
uncertainty surrounds the status of blacks between the founding
of Jamestown (1607) and the sixties. Oscar and Mary Handlin
contend that in the beginning Virginia and Maryland treated
blacks much like white indentured servants. To attract more
white immigrants, their masters gave white servants more
freedom toward the middle of the seventeenth century. The
blacks, on the other hand, were gradually enslaved. Only after
enslavement did the slaveholders employ the doctrine of black
racial inferiority to justify the difference. In short, slavery
preceded prejudice. In Degler's selection he argues that the
Africans were victims of discrimination in length of service,
carrying firearms, punishment, manumission, and marriage. But
Winthrop D. Jordan finds that the existing evidence fails to
support the conclusions of either the Handlins or Degler. He
maintains that enslavement and other forms of discrimination
occurred simultaneously as part of a general debasement of the
blacks. Is the confusion over the relationship between the origins

of slavery and the development of prejudice a product of improperly defined terms? Since slavery had existed in Spanish America and Brazil before 1607, how relevant are some of these speculations about the beginnings of slavery in the American colonies?

James Ford Rhodes and Ulrich B. Phillips in the next unit offer both the traditional attack upon slavery and the defense of the institution. Before the war most of the material by the abolitionists and proslavery advocates was polemical. Not until emancipation did it become possible to consider the question with detachment. Such was Rhodes's purpose in writing his *History of the United States from the Compromise of 1850*. He repeated Henry Clay's verdict: "Slavery is a curse to the master and a wrong to the slave." While making clear his opinion of the intellectual and moral capabilities of the blacks, Rhodes drew a devastating and detailed picture of slavery as an example of man's inhumanity to man. Is this interpretation—that slavery was a curse, when so many profited, and yet a wrong to the slave whom he defined as inferior—enigmatic? In contrast Phillips depicts slavery as essentially a kind and paternal system with contented slaves; the plantation was a school adjusting a backward and childlike people to the standards of a higher civilization. While Phillips did not use those sources that did not confirm his view of plantation life and the slaves as docile, fun loving, and happy, his studies and monographs have had a substantial impact upon twentieth-century historical thought. Since 1945 the revisionist writers have questioned his methods, interpretations, and views.

The psychological effects of bondage upon the slave psyche are analyzed in Part III by Stanley Elkins, Kenneth M. Stampp, and Sterling Stuckey. Until the publication of Elkins's *Slavery: A Problem in American Institutional and Intellectual Life* (1959), historians had not considered the personality-distorting potential of bondage. To Elkins, the Sambo stereotype—the childlike, loyal slave—represents not a myth but an actuality. This personality type was the result of a totally closed institution, slavery, acting upon a personality, denying the slave a life-style or set of values other than that prescribed by the master. *Slavery* ranks as a pioneer work in the use of interdisciplinary techniques from social psychology, anthropology, and economics. Elkins's use of these disciplines comes out in his analogy between the Sambo stereotype and the inmates of German concentration camps. Are there sufficient similarities between a slave plantation and a concentration camp to justify the analogy? Stampp, in his selection, does not think so and points to the lack of empirical evidence to back up Elkins's assertion of the widespread existence of a Sambo type. In contrast, and using a different approach, Stuckey shows that the slaves were able to develop a life-style and a set of values different from the desires of their masters and one which provided a positive self-image and non-Sambo personality. Black folklore and songs are the bases for his interpretation.

In the next section the question of slave resistance is explored by Raymond and Alice Bauer and Vincent Harding. Resistance to the Axis powers during World War II was probably the catalyst for these and other studies attacking the docile slave portrait of plantation life by emphasizing antebellum slave revolts and slave disloyalty during the Civil War. Yet revolts were not the only forms of resistance. Raymond and Alice Bauer give examples of work slowdowns, the destruction of farm equipment, the feigning of illness, and the injuring of farm animals; there may have been others. How widespread this type of resistance was requires further research.

Interpretations of the relationship between religion and the slave have depicted Christianity as a way, an instrument, of plantation management in encouraging slave docility and passivity. Religion would function as "the opium of the people," providing immediate gratification and negating the discontent so necessary to initiate change. Harding in his selection offers a different argument. Slaves identified their plight with the persecution of the Israelites and their attempts to overthrow their oppressors. Even though efficient plantation management dictated the isolation of blacks from abolitionist propaganda and contacts with free slaves, the blacks interpreted Christianity in terms of their own interest.

Slavery had a significance to the nation beyond the questions of resistance and the effects upon personality. Slavery involved the North and the South in our bloodiest war; why is a constant and perplexing question. Expansion of slavery and its profits are the topics considered in Part V as reasons precipitating the Civil War. Charles W. Ramsdell shows that the sectional controversy over the expansion of slavery was a hollow issue. Soil exhaustion would have made it unprofitable, and the climate and geography of the West were not hospitable. These arguments are not accepted by Eugene D. Genovese who maintains that the planter class was an anticapitalistic group, ideologically committed to slavery as a way of life morally superior to the ruthless capitalism of the North. Genovese suggests that slaves could have been used in the western territories—in farming and mining. Robert S. Starobin substantiates this argument by showing that a campaign to use slaves in southern industries was underway in the 1840s and 1850s. The movement for slave-based industries paralleled the abolitionist attacks. By 1861 the campaign for slave-based industries and southern nationalism was entwined in the movement for secession. But if the ruling class was willing to industrialize, does the depth of their commitment to Genovese's anticapitalistic agrarian society weaken and the possibility of the South evolving to resemble the capitalist nonslave North increase?

In the final group of readings, Stanley Elkins and David Brion Davis are concerned with the differences between slavery in the United States and in Latin America and the effects upon the two multiracial societies. In a pioneering study, *Slave and Citizen: The Negro in the Americas* (1947), Frank Tannenbaum put forth the view that the history of the black man in the New World was structured differently in the United States from that in the Spanish and Portuguese areas. He emphasized that when the law recognized the "moral personality" of the slave—his right to marriage, family, and property—and made the achievement of freedom relatively easy, as it did in Latin America, slavery was abolished without force. Elkins's selection points out that the centralization of secular authority in the Spanish and Portuguese monarchies, and religious authority in the Catholic church made possible the curtailment of brutal treatment and violations against the slave's moral personality. In direct contrast, Davis concludes that Spanish and Portuguese attitudes and actions differed little from those in the United States. The Tannenbaum-Elkins interpretation, according to Davis, mistakenly accepts their legal codes as a literal description of the conditions of Latin American slavery. One should consider whether Davis's decision to compare the colonial period of Latin American slavery with the institution as it existed in nineteenth-century United States weakens his challenge to Elkins.

The debate over the nature and effects of slavery is a continuing controversy. More research into the primary sources will provide answers to some of the questions. Certainly more inquiry is needed into Afro-American folklore, slave songs, and oral tradition before the effects of bondage upon personality and behavior are known. Research on the origins of slavery and racism point out the necessity for psychologically oriented studies. Future comparative studies on North American and Latin American slavery must consider regional variations and their relationship to the history of the respective mother countries. In the process of providing answers to existing questions about slavery, historians will raise new ones.

These readings touch only the fringes of the mass of literature that is available. Suggestions for additional readings upon all the subjects are given in the bibliography.

part one
the origins of slavery

one
on the road
to enslavement

OSCAR AND MARY HANDLIN

Oscar Handlin (b. 1915) is Charles Warren Professor of History at Harvard University. Born in New York City and educated through the New York public school system, he did his graduate work at Harvard where he received his M.A. and Ph.D. (1940). One of his major fields of study is European immigrants and their adjustments to American society. Two of his works in this area have achieved special recognition–Boston's Immigrants received the Dunning Prize from the American History Association in 1941 and The Uprooted won the Pulitzer Prize in history in 1952. Mary Handlin (b. 1913), collaborator and wife of Oscar Handlin, is a research editor at the Center for the Study of the History of Liberty in America. She received her B.A. from Brooklyn College and M.A. from Columbia University. She has coauthored with Oscar Handlin: Commonwealth: A Study of the Role of Government in American Economy*;* Dimensions of Liberty*; and* Popular Sources of Political Authority.

Through the first three-quarters of the seventeenth century, the Negroes, even in the South, were not numerous; nor were they particularly concentrated in any district. They came into a society in which a large part of the population was to some degree unfree; indeed in Virginia under the Company almost everyone, even tenants and laborers, bore some sort of servile obligation. The Negroes' lack of freedom was not unusual. These newcomers, like so many others, were accepted, bought and held, as kinds of servants. They were certainly not well off. But their

Source: Oscar and Mary Handlin, "Origins of the Southern Labor System," reprinted in Oscar Handlin, *Race and Nationality in American Life* (Boston: Little, Brown, 1957), pp. 6–18. Without footnotes. Copyright © 1950, 1957 by Oscar Handlin. Reprinted by permission of Atlantic-Little, Brown, and Co.

ill-fortune was of a sort they shared with men from England, Scotland,
and Ireland, and with the unlucky aborigenes held in captivity. Like the others,
some Negroes became free, that is, terminated their period of service. Some
became artisans; a few became landowners and the masters of other men. The status of
Negroes was that of servants; and so they were identified and treated down to the
1660's.

The word, "slave" was, of course, used occasionally. It had no meaning in English
law, but there was a significant colloquial usage. This was a general term of derogation.
It served to express contempt; "O what a rogue and peasant slave am I," says Hamlet
(Act II, Scene 2). It also described the low-born as contrasted with the gentry; of two
hundred warriors, a sixteenth-century report said, eight were gentlemen, the rest slaves.
The implication of degradation was also transferred to the low kinds of labor; "In this
hal," wrote More (1551), "all vyle seruice, all slauerie . . . is done by bondemen."

It was in this sense that Negro servants were sometimes called slaves. But the same
appelation was, in England, given to other non-English servants,—to a Russian, for
instance. In Europe and in the American colonies, the term was, at various times and
places, applied indiscriminately to Indians, mulattoes, and mestizos, as well as to
Negroes. For that matter, it applied also to white Englishmen. It thus commonly
described the servitude of children; so, the poor planters complained, "Our children, the
parents dieinge" are held as "slaues or drudges" for the discharge of their parents' debts.
Penal servitude too was often referred to as slavery; and the phrase, "slavish servant"
turns up from time to time. Slavery had no meaning in law; at most it was a popular
description of a low form of service.

Yet in not much more than a half century after 1660 this term of derogation was
transformed into a fixed legal position. In a society characterized by many degrees of
unfreedom, the Negro fell into a status novel to English law, into an unknown
condition toward which the colonists unsteadily moved, slavery in its eighteenth- and
nineteenth-century form. The available accounts do not explain this development
because they assume that this form of slavery was known from the start.

Can it be said, for instance, that the seventeenth-century Englishman might have
discovered elsewhere an established institution, the archetype of slavery as it was
ultimately defined, which seemed more advantageous than the defined English customs
for use in the New World? The internationally recognized "slave trade" has been cited
as such an institution. But when one notes that the Company of Royal Adventurers
referred to their cargo as "Negers," "Negro-Servants," "Servants . . . from Africa," or
"Negro Person," but rarely as slaves, it is not so clear that it had in view some unique
or different status. And when one remembers that the transportation of Irish servants
was also known as the "slave-trade," then it is clear that those who sold and those who
bought the Negro, if they troubled to consider legal status at all, still thought of him
simply as a low servant.

Again, it has been assumed that Biblical and Roman law offered adequate precedent.
But it did not seem so in the perspective of the contemporaries of the first planters who
saw in both the Biblical and Roman institutions simply the equivalents of their own
familiar forms of servitude. King James's translators rendered the word, "bond-servant";

"slave" does not appear in their version. And to Coke the Roman *servus* was no more than the villein ("and this is hee which the civilians call servus").

Nor did the practice of contemporary Europeans fall outside the English conceptions of servitude. Since early in the fifteenth century, the Portuguese had held Moors, white and black, in "slavery," at home, on the Atlantic islands, and in Brazil. Such servitude also existed in Spain and in Spanish America where Negroes were eagerly imported to supply the perennial shortage of labor in the Caribbean sugar islands and the Peruvian mines. But what was the status of such slaves? They had certain property rights, were capable of contracting marriages, and were assured of the integrity of their families. Once baptised it was almost a matter of course that they would become free; the right to manumission was practically a "contractual arrangement." And once free, they readily intermarried with their former masters. These were no chattels, devoid of personality. These were human beings whom chance had rendered unfree, a situation completely comprehensible within the degrees of unfreedom familiar to the English colonist. Indeed when Bodin wishes to illustrate the condition of such "slaves," he refers to servants and apprentices in England and Scotland.

Finally, there is no basis for the assertion that such a colony as South Carolina simply adopted slavery from the French or British West Indies. To begin with, the labor system of those places was not yet fully evolved. Travelers from the mainland may have noted the advantages of Negro labor there; but they hardly thought of chattel slavery. The Barbadian gentlemen who proposed to come to South Carolina in 1663 thought of bringing "Negros and other servants." They spoke of "slaves" as did other Englishmen, as a low form of servant; the "weaker" servants to whom the Concessions referred included "woemen children slaves." Clearly American slavery was no direct imitation from Biblical or Roman or Spanish or Portuguese or West Indian models. Whatever connections existed were established in the eighteenth and nineteenth centuries when those who justified the emerging institution cast about for possible precedents wherever they might be found.

If chattel slavery was not present from the start, nor adopted from elsewhere, it was also not a response to any inherent qualities that fitted the Negro for plantation labor. There has been a good deal of speculation as to the relative efficiency of free and slave, of Negro, white, and Indian, labor. Of necessity, estimates of which costs were higher, which risks—through mortality, escape, and rebellion—greater, are inconclusive. What is conclusive is the fact that Virginia and Maryland planters did not think Negro labor more desirable. A preference for white servants persisted even on the islands. But when the Barbadians could not get those, repeated representations in London made known their desire for Negroes. No such demands came from the continental colonies. On the contrary the calls are for skilled white labor with the preference for those most like the first settlers and ranging down from Scots and Welsh to Irish, French, and Italians. Least desired were the unskilled, utterly strange Negroes.

It is quite clear in fact that as late as 1669 those who thought of large scale agriculture assumed it would be manned not by Negroes but by white peasants under a condition of villeinage. John Locke's constitutions for South Carolina envisaged an hereditary group of servile "leetmen"; and Lord Shaftsbury's signory on Locke Island in

1674 actually attempted to put that scheme into practice. If the holders of large estates in the Chesapeake colonies expressed no wish for a Negro labor supply, they could hardly have planned to use black hands as a means of displacing white, whether as a concerted plot by restoration courtiers to set up a new social order in America, or as a program for lowering costs.

Yet the Negroes did cease to be servants and became slaves, ceased to be men in whom masters held a proprietary interest and became chattels, objects that were the property of their owners. In that transformation originated the southern labor system.

Although the colonists assumed at the start that all servants would "fare alike in the colony," the social realities of their situation early gave rise to differences of treatment. It is not necessary to resort to racialist assumptions to account for such measures; these were simply the reactions of immigrants lost to the stability and security of home and isolated in an immense wilderness in which threats from the unknown were all about them. Like the millions who would follow, these immigrants longed in the strangeness for the company of familiar men and singled out to be welcomed those who were most like themselves. So the measures regulating settlement spoke specifically in this period of differential treatment for various groups. From time to time, regulations applied only to "those of our own nation," or to the French, the Dutch, the Italians, the Swiss, the Palatines, the Welsh, the Irish, or to combinations of the diverse nationalities drawn to these shores.

In the same way the colonists became aware of the differences between themselves and the African immigrants. The rudeness of the Negroes' manners, the strangeness of their languages, the difficulty of communicating to them English notions of morality and proper behavior occasioned sporadic laws to regulate their conduct. So, Bermuda's law to restrain the insolencies of Negroes "who are servents" (that is, their inclination to run off with the pigs of others) was the same in kind as the legislation that the Irish should "straggle not night or dai, as it too common with them." Until the 1660's the statutes on the Negroes were not at all unique. Nor did they add up to a decided trend.

But in the decade after 1660 far more significant differentiations with regard to term of service, relationship to Christianity, and disposal of children, cut the Negro apart from all other servants and gave a new depth to his bondage.

In the early part of the century duration of service was of only slight importance. Certainly in England where labor was more plentiful than the demand, expiration of a term had little meaning; the servant was free only to enter upon another term, while the master had always the choice of taking on the old or a new servitor. That situation obtained even in America as long as starvation was a real possibility. In 1621, it was noted, "vittles being scarce in the country noe man will tacke servants." As late as 1643 Lord Baltimore thought it better if possible to hire labor than to risk the burden of supporting servants through a long period. Under such conditions the number of years specified in the indenture was not important, and if a servant had no indenture the question was certainly not likely to rise.

That accounts for the early references to unlimited service. Thus Sandys's plan for Virginia in 1618 spoke of tenants-at-half assigned to the treasurer's office, to "belong to said office for ever." Again, those at Berkeley's Hundred were perpetual "after the manner of estates in England." Since perpetual in seventeenth-century law meant that which had "not any set time expressly allotted for [its] . . . continuance," such provisions were not surprising. Nor was it surprising to find instances in the court records of Negroes who seemed to serve forever. These were quite compatible with the possibility of ultimate freedom. Thus a colored man bought in 1644 "as a Slave for Ever," nevertheless was held "to serve as other Christians servants do" and freed after a term.

The question of length of service became critical when the mounting value of labor eased the fear that servants would be a drain on "vittles" and raised the expectation of profit from their toil. Those eager to multiply the number of available hands by stimulating immigration had not only to overcome the reluctance of a prospective newcomer faced with the trials of a sea journey; they had also to counteract the widespread reports in England and Scotland that servants were harshly treated and bound in perpetual slavery.

To encourage immigration therefore, the colonies embarked upon a line of legislation designed to improve servants' conditions and to enlarge the prospect of a meaningful release, a release that was not the start of a new period of servitude, but of life as a freeman and landowner. Thus Virginia, in 1642, discharged "publick tenants from their servitudes, who, like one sort of villians anciently in England" were attached to the lands of the governor; and later laws provided that no person was to "be adjudged to serve the collonie hereafter." Most significant were the statutes which reassured prospective newcomers by setting limits to the terms of servants without indentures, in 1638/9 in Maryland, in 1642/3 in Virginia. These acts seem to have applied only to voluntary immigrants "of our own nation." The Irish and other aliens, less desirable, at first received longer terms. But the realization that such discrimination retarded "the peopling of the country" led to an extension of the identical privilege to all Christians.

But the Negro never profited from these enactments. Farthest removed from the English, least desired, he communicated with no friends who might be deterred from following. Since his coming was involuntary, nothing that happened to him would increase or decrease his numbers. To raise the status of Europeans by shortening their terms would ultimately increase the available hands by inducing their compatriots to emigrate; to reduce the Negro's term would produce an immediate loss and no ultimate gain. By midcentury the servitude of Negroes seems generally lengthier than that of whites; and thereafter the consciousness dawns that the Blacks will toil for the whole of their lives, not through any particular concern with their status but simply by contrast with those whose years of labor are limited by statute. The legal position of the Negro is, however, still uncertain; it takes legislative action to settle that.

The Maryland House, complaining of that ambiguity, provoked the decisive measure; "All Negroes and other slaues," it was enacted, "shall serve Durante Vita." Virginia reached the same end more tortuously. An act of 1661 had assumed, in imposing penalties on runaways, that *some* Negroes served for life. The law of 1670 went further; "all servants not being christians" brought in by sea were declared slaves for life.

But slavery for life was still tenuous as long as the slave could extricate himself by baptism. The fact that Negroes were heathens had formerly justified their bondage, since infidels were "perpetual" enemies of Christians. It had followed that conversion was a way to freedom. Governor Archdale thus released the Spanish Indians captured to be sold as slaves to Jamaica when he learned they were Christians. As labor rose in value this presumption dissipated the zeal of masters for proselytizing. So that they be "freed from this doubt" a series of laws between 1667 and 1671 laid down the rule that conversion alone did not lead to a release from servitude. Thereafter manumission, which other servants could demand by right at the end of their terms, in the case of Negroes lay entirely within the discretion of the master.

A difference in the status of the offspring of Negro and white servants followed inevitably from the differentiation in the length of their terms. The problem of disposing of the issue of servants was at first general. Bastardy, prevalent to begin with and more frequent as the century advanced, deprived the master of his women's work and subjected him to the risk of their death. Furthermore the parish was burdened with the support of the child. The usual procedure was to punish the offenders with fines or whippings and to compel the servant to serve beyond his time for the benefit of the parish and to recompense the injured master.

The general rule ceased to apply once the Negro was bound for life, for there was no means of extending his servitude. The most the outraged master could get was the child, a minimal measure of justice, somewhat tempered by the trouble of rearing the infant to an age of usefulness. The truly vexing problem was to decide on the proper course when one parent was free, for it was not certain whether the English law that the issue followed the state of the father would apply. Maryland, which adopted that rule in 1664, found that unscrupulous masters instigated intercourse between their Negro males and white females which not only gave them the offspring, but, to boot, the service of the woman for the life of her husband. The solution in Virginia which followed the precedent of the bastardy laws and had the issue follow the mother seemed preferable and ultimately was adopted in Maryland and elsewhere.

By the last quarter of the seventeenth century, one could distinguish clearly between the Negro slave who served for life and the servant for a period. But there was not yet a demarcation in personal terms: the servant was not yet a free man, nor the slave a chattel. As late as 1686, the words slave and servant could still be conflated to an extent that indicated men conceived of them as extensions of the same condition. A Frenchman in Virginia in that year noted, "There are degrees among the slaves brought here, for a Christian over 21 years of age cannot be held a slave more than five years, but the negroes and other infidels remain slaves all their lives."

It was the persistence of such conceptions that raised the fear that "noe free borne Christians will ever be induced to come over servants" without overwhelming assurance that there would be nothing slavish in their lot. After all Pennsylvania and New York now gave the European newcomer a choice of destination. In Virginia and Maryland there was a persistent effort to make immigration more attractive by further ameliorating the lot of European servants. The custom of the country undoubtedly moved more rapidly than the letter of the law. "Weake and Ignorant" juries on which former servants sat often decided cases against masters. But even the letter of the law showed a noticeable decline in the use of the death penalty and in the power of masters over men. By 1705 in some colonies, white servants were no longer transferable; they could not be whipped without a court order; and they were protected against the avaricious unreasonable masters who attempted to force them into new contracts "some small tyme before the expiration of their tyme of service."

Meanwhile the condition of the Negro deteriorated. In these very years, a startling growth in numbers complicated the problem. The Royal African Company was, to some extent, responsible, though its operations in the mainland colonies formed only a very minor part of its business. But the opening of Africa to free trade in 1698 inundated Virginia, Maryland, and South Carolina with new slaves. Under the pressure of policing these newcomers the regulation of Negroes actually grew harsher.

The early laws against runaways, against drunkenness, against carrying arms or trading without permission had applied penalties as heavy as death to all servants, Negroes and whites. But these regulations grew steadily less stringent in the case of white servants. On the other hand fear of the growing number of slaves, uneasy suspicion of plots and conspiracies, led to more stringent control of Negroes and a broad view of the master's power of discipline. Furthermore the emerging difference in treatment was calculated to create a real division of interest between Negroes on the one hand and whites on the other. Servants who ran away in the company of slaves, for instance, were doubly punished, for the loss of their own time and for the time of the slaves, a provision that discouraged such joint ventures. Similarly Negroes, even when freed, retained some disciplinary links with their less fortunate fellows. The wardens continued to supervise their children, they were not capable of holding white servants, and serious restrictions limited the number of manumissions.

The growth of the Negro population also heightened the old concern over sexual immorality and the conditions of marriage. The law had always recognized the interest of the lord in the marriage of his villein or neife and had frowned on the mixed marriage of free and unfree. Similarly it was inclined to hold that the marriage of any servant was a loss to the master, an "Enormious offense" productive of much detriment "against the law of God," and therefore dependent on the consent of the master. Mixed marriages of free men and servants were particularly frowned upon as complicating status and therefore limited by law.

There was no departure from these principles in the early cases of Negro-white relationships. Even the complicated laws of Maryland in 1664 and the manner of their enactment revealed no change in attitude. The marriage of Blacks and whites was possible; what was important was the status of the partners and of their issue. It was to guard against the complications of status that the laws after 1691 forbade "spurious" or illegitimate mixed marriages of the slave and the free and punished violations with heavy penalties. Yet it was also significant that by then the prohibition was couched in terms, not simply of slave and free man, but of Negro and white. Here was evidence as in the policing regulations of an emerging demarkation.

The first settlers in Virginia had been concerned with the difficulty of preserving the solidarity of the group under the disruptive effects of migration. They had been enjoined to "keepe to themselves" not to "marry nor give in marriage to the heathen, that are uncircumcised." But such resolutions were difficult to maintain and had gradually relaxed until the colonists included among "themselves" such groups as the Irish, once the objects of very general contempt. A common lot drew them together; and it was the absence of a common lot that drew these apart from the Negro. At the opening of the eighteenth century, the Black was not only set off by economic and legal status; he was "abominable," another order of man.

Yet the ban on intermarriage did not rest on any principle of white racial purity, for many men contemplated with equanimity the prospect of amalgamation with the Indians. That did not happen, for the mass of Redmen were free to recede into the interior while those who remained sank into slavery as abject as that of the Blacks and intermarried with those whose fate they shared.

Color then emerged as the token of the slave status; the trace of color became the trace of slavery. It had not always been so; as late as the 1660's the law had not even a word to describe the children of mixed marriages. But two decades later, the term mulatto is used, and it serves, not as in Brazil, to whiten the Black, but to affiliate through the color tie the offspring of a spurious union with his inherited slavery. (The compiler of the Virginia laws then takes the liberty of altering the texts to bring earlier legislation into line with his own new notions.) Ultimately the complete judicial doctrine begins to show forth, a slave cannot be a white man, and every man of color was descendent of a slave.

The rising wall dividing the legal status of the slave from that of the servant was buttressed by other developments which derogated the qualities of the Negro as a human being to establish his inferiority and thus completed his separation from the white. The destruction of the black man's personality involved, for example, a peculiar style of designation. In the seventeenth century many immigrants in addition to the Africans—Swedes, Armenians, Jews—had brought no family names to America. By the eighteenth all but the Negroes had acquired them. In the seventeenth century, Indians and Negroes bore names that were either an approximation of their original ones or similar to those of their masters—Diana, Jane, Frank, Juno, Anne, Maria, Jenny. In the eighteenth century slaves seem increasingly to receive classical or biblical appelations, by analogy with Roman and Hebrew bondsmen. Deprivation by statute and usage of other civic rights, to vote, to testify, to bring suit, even if free, completed the process. And after 1700 appear the full slave codes, formal recognition that the Negroes are not governed by the laws of other men.

The identical steps that made the slave less a man made him more a chattel. All servants had once been reckoned property of a sort; a runaway was guilty of "Stealth of ones self." Negroes were then no different from others. But every law that improved the condition of the white servant chipped away at the property element in his status. The growing emphasis upon the consent of the servant, upon the limits of his term, upon the obligations to him, and upon the conditional nature of his dependence, steadily converted the relationship from an ownership to a contractual basis. None of these considerations applied to the Negro; on the contrary considerations of consent and conditions disappeared from his life. What was left was his status as property—in most cases a chattel though for special purposes real estate.

two
slavery and the
genesis of american
race prejudice

CARL N. DEGLER

Carl N. Degler (b. 1921) is author of the widely acclaimed Out of
Our Past: The Forces that Shaped Modern America. *On the
question of slavery and prejudice, he finds the assumptions of some
historians that enslavement was responsible for prejudice against blacks
open to debate. In this essay, convinced that prejudice predated slavery,
he argues that whites and blacks were treated differently from the
earliest days of the colonial period. More recently Professor Degler has
been looking at the problem from another angle by making a
comparative study of slavery in Brazil and the United States. Before
going to Stanford University, he taught at Vassar College from 1952 to
1968.*

It is indeed true as the Handlins in their article have emphasized
that before the seventeenth century the Negro was rarely called a
slave. But this fact should not overshadow the historical evidence
which points to the institution without employing the name.
Because no discriminatory title is placed upon the Negro we
must not think that he was being treated like a white servant; for
there is too much evidence to the contrary. Although the growth
of a fully developed slave law was slow, unsteady and often
unarticulated in surviving records, this is what one would expect
when an institution is first being worked out. It is not the same,
however, as saying that no slavery or discrimination against the
Negro existed in the first decades of the Negro's history in America.

Source: Carl N. Degler, "Slavery and the Genesis of American Race Prejudice,"
Comparative Studies in Society and History (October 1959): 55–62. Reprinted by
permission of the Cambridge University Press.

As will appear from the evidence which follows, the kinds of discrimination visited upon Negroes varied immensely. In the early 1640's it sometimes stopped short of lifetime servitude or inheritable status—the two attributes of true slavery—in other instances it included both. But regardless of the form of discrimination, the important point is that from the 1630's up until slavery clearly appeared in the statutes in the 1660s, the Negroes were being set apart and discriminated against as compared with the treatment accorded Englishmen, whether servants or free.

The colonists of the early seventeenth century were well aware of a distinction between indentured servitude and slavery. This is quite clear from the evidence in the very early years of the century. The most obvious means the English colonists had for learning of a different treatment for Negroes from that for white servants was the slave trade and the slave systems of the Spanish and Portuguese colonies. As early as 1623, a voyager's book published in London indicated that Englishmen knew of the Negro as a slave in the South American colonies of Spain. The book told of the trade in "blacke people" who were "sold unto the Spaniard for him to carry into the West Indies, to remaine as slaves, either in their Mines or in any other servile uses, they in those countries put them to". In the phrase "remaine as slaves" is the element of unlimited service.

The Englishmen's treatment of another dark-skinned, non-Christian people—the Indians—further supports the argument that a special and inferior status was accorded the Negro virtually from the first arrival. Indian slavery was practised in all of the English settlements almost from the beginning and, though it received its impetus from the perennial wars between the races, the fact that an inferior and onerous service was established for the Indian makes it plausible to suppose that a similar status would be reserved for the equally different and pagan Negro.

The continental English could also draw upon other models of a differentiated status for Negroes. The earliest English colony to experiment with large numbers of Negroes in its midst was the shortlived settlement of Providence island, situated in the western Caribbean, just off the Mosquito Coast. By 1637, long before Barbados and the other British sugar islands utilized great numbers of Negroes, almost half of the population of this Puritan venture was black. Such a disproportion of races caused great alarm among the directors of the Company in London and repeated efforts were made to restrict the influx of blacks. Partly because of its large numbers of Negroes, Old Providence became well known to the mainland colonies of Virginia and New England. A. P. Newton has said that Old Providence

> . . . *forms the connecting link between almost every English colonising enterprise in the first half of the seventeenth century from Virginia and Bermuda to New England and Jamaica, and thus it is of much greater importance than its actual accomplishments would justify.*

Under such circumstances, it was to be expected that knowledge of the status accorded Negroes by these Englishmen would be transmitted to those on the mainland with whom they had such close and frequent contact.

Though the word "slave" is never applied to the Negroes on Providence, and only rarely the word "Servant", "Negroes", which was the term used, were obviously *sui generis;* they were people apart from the English. The Company, for example, distrusted them. "Association [Tortuga island] was deserted thro' their mutinous conduct", the Company told the Governor of Old Providence in 1637. "Further trade for them prohibited, with exceptions, until Providence be furnished with English." In another communication the Company again alluded to the dangers of "too great a number" of Negroes on the island and promised to send 200 English servants over to be exchanged for as many Negroes. A clearer suggestion of the difference in status between an English servant and a Negro is contained in the Company's letter announcing the forwarding of the 200 servants. As a further precaution against being overwhelmed by Negroes, it was ordered that a "family of fourteen"—which would include servants—was not to have more than six Negroes. "The surplusage may be sold to the poor men who have served their apprenticeship". But the Negroes, apparently, were serving for life.

Other British island colonies in the seventeenth century also provide evidence which is suggestive of this same development of a differing status for Negroes, even though the word "slave" was not always employed. Though apparently the first Negroes were only brought to Bermuda in 1617, as early as 1623 the Assembly passed an "Act to restrayne the insolencies of Negroes". The blacks were accused of stealing and of carrying "secretly cudgels, and other weapons and working tools". Such weapons, it was said, were "very dangerous and not meete to be suffered to be carried by such Vassals. . . ." Already, in other words, Negroes were treated as a class apart. To reinforce this, Negroes were forbidden to "weare any weapon in the daytyme" and they were not to be outside or off their master's land during "any undue hours in the night tyme . . .".

During the 1630's there were other indications that Negroes were treated as inferiors. As early as 1630 some Negroes' servitude was already slavery in that it was for life and inheritable. One Lew Forde possessed a Negro man, while the Company owned his wife; the couple had two children. Forde desired "to know which of the said children properly belong to himself and which to the Company". The Council gave him the older child and the Company received the other. A letter of Roger Wood in 1634 suggests that Negroes were already serving for life, for he asked to have a Negro, named Sambo, given to him, so that through the Negro "I or myne may *ever* be able" to carry on an old feud with an enemy who owned Sambo's wife.

There is further evidence of discrimination against Negroes in later years. A grand jury in 1652 cited one Henry Gaunt as being "suspected of being unnecessarily conversant with negro women"—he had been giving them presents. The presentment added that "if he hath not left his familiarity with such creatures, it is desired that such abominations be inquired into, least the land mourne for them". The discrimination reached a high point in 1656 when the Governor proclaimed that "any Englishman" who discovered a Negro walking about at night without a pass, was empowered to "kill him then and theire without mercye". The proclamation further ordered that all free Negroes "shall be banished from these Islands, never to return eyther by purchase of any man, or otherwise . . .". When some Negroes asked the Governor for their freedom in 1669, he denied they had any such claim, saying that they had been "purchased by" their masters "without condition or limitation. It being likewise soe practised in these American plantations and other parts of the world."

In Barbados Negroes were already slaves when Richard Ligon lived there in 1647–50. "The Iland", he later wrote, "is divided into three sorts of men, viz: Masters, servants, and slaves. The slaves and their posterity, being subject to their masters for ever," in contrast to the servants who are owned "but for five years . . .". On that island as at Bermuda it was reported that Negroes were not permitted "to touch or handle any weapons".

On Jamaica, as on the other two islands, a clear distinction was made between the status of the Negro and that of the English servant. In 1656 one resident of the island wrote the Protector in England urging the importation of African Negroes because then, he said, "the planters would have to pay for them" and therefore "they would have an interest in preserving their lives, *which was* wanting in the case of bond servants . . .".

It is apparent, then, that the colonists on the mainland had ample opportunity before 1660 to learn of a different status for black men from that for Englishmen, whether servants or free.

From the evidence available it would seem that the Englishmen in Virginia and Maryland learned their lesson well. This is true even though the sources available on the Negro's position in these colonies in the early years are not as abundant as we would like. It seems quite evident that the black man was set apart from the white on the continent just as he was being set apart in the island colonies. For example, in Virginia in 1630, one Hugh Davis was "soundly whipped before an Assembly of Negroes and others for abusing himself to the dishonor of God and the shame of Christians, by defiling his body in lying with a negro". The unChristian-like character of such behavior was emphasized ten years later when Robert Sweet was ordered to do penance in Church for "getting a negro woman with child". An act passed in the Maryland legislature in 1639 indicated that at that early date the word "slave" was being applied to non-Englishmen. The act was an enumeration of the rights of "all Christian inhabitants (slaves excepted)". The slaves referred to could have been only Indians or Negroes, since all white servants were Christians. It is also significant of the differing treatment of the two races that though Maryland and Virginia very early in their history enacted laws fixing limits to the terms for servants who entered without written contracts, Negroes were never included in such protective provisions. The first of such laws were placed upon the books in 1639 in Maryland and 1643 in Virginia; in the Maryland statute, it was explicitly stated: "Slaves excepted".

In yet another way, Negroes and slaves were singled out for special status in the years before 1650. A Virginia law of 1640 provided that "all masters" should try to furnish arms to themselves and "all those of their families which shall be capable of arms"—which would include servants—"(excepting negroes)". Not until 1648 did Maryland get around to such a prohibition, when it was provided that no guns should be given to "any Pagan for killing meate or to any other use", upon pain of a heavy fine. At no time were white servants denied the right to bear arms; indeed, as these statutes inform us, they were enjoined to possess weapons.

One other class of discriminatory acts against Negroes in Virginia and Maryland before 1660 also deserves to be noticed. Three different times before 1660—in 1643, 1644 and 1658—the Virginia assembly (and in 1654, the Maryland legislature) included Negro and Indian women among the "tithables". But white servant women were never placed in such a category, inasmuch as they were not expected to work in the fields. From the beginning, it would seem, Negro women, whether free or bond, were treated by the law differently from white women servants.

It is not until the 1640's that evidence of a status for Negroes akin to slavery, and, therefore, something more than mere discrimination begins to appear in the sources. Two cases of punishment for runaway servants in 1640 throw some light on the working out of a differentiated status for Negroes. The first case concerned three runaways, of whom two were white men and the third a Negro. All three were given thirty lashes, with the white men having the terms owed their masters extended a year, at the completion of which they were to work for the colony for three more years. The other, "being a Negro named John Punch shall serve his said master or his assigns for the time of his natural Life here or elsewhere". Not only was the Negro's punishment the most severe, and for no apparent reason, but he was, in effect, reduced to slavery. It is also clear, however, that up until the issuing of the sentence, he must have had the status of a servant.

The second case, also of 1640, suggests that by that date some Negroes were already slaves. Six white men and a Negro were implicated in a plot to run away. The punishments meted out varied, but Christopher Miller "a dutchman" (a prime agent in the business) "was given the harshest treatment of all: thirty stripes, burning with an "R" on the cheek, a shackle placed on his leg for a year "and longer if said master shall see cause" and seven years of service for the colony upon completion of his time due his master. The only other one of the seven plotters to receive the stripes, the shackle and the "R" was the Negro Emanuel, but, significantly, he did not receive any sentence of work for the colony. Presumably he was already serving his master for a life-time—*i.e.,* he was a slave. About this time in Maryland it does not seem to have been unusual to speak of Negroes as slaves, for in 1642 one "John Skinner mariner" agreed "to deliver unto . . . Leonard Calvert, fourteen negro-men-slaves and three women-slaves".

From a proceeding before the House of Burgesses in 1666 it appears that as early as 1644 that body was being called upon to determine who was a slave. The Journal of the House for 1666 reports that in 1644 a certain "mulata" bought "as a slave for Ever" was adjudged by the Assembly "no slave and but to serve as other Christian servants do" and was freed in September 1665. Though no reason was given for the verdict, from the words "other Christian servants" it is possible that he was a Christian, for it was believed in the early years of the English colonies that baptism rendered a slave free. In any case, the Assembly uttered no prohibition of slavery as such and the owner was sufficiently surprised and aggrieved by the decision to appeal for recompense from the Assembly, even though the Negro's service was twenty-one years, an unheard of term for a "Christian servant".

In early seventeenth century inventories of estates, there are two distinctions which appear in the reckoning of the value of servants and Negroes. Uniformly, the Negroes were more valuable, even as children, than any white servant. Secondly, the naming of a servant is usually followed by the number of years yet remaining to his service; for the

Negroes no such notation appears. Thus in an inventory in Virginia in 1643, a 22-year old white servant, with eight years still to serve, was valued at 1,000 pounds of tobacco, while a "negro boy" was rated at 3,000 pounds and a white boy with seven years to serve was listed as worth 700 pounds. An eight-year old Negro girl was calculated to be worth 2,000 pounds. On another inventory in 1655, two good men servants with four years to serve were rated at 1,300 pounds of tobacco, and a woman servant with only two years to go was valued at 800 pounds. Two Negro boys, however, who had no limit set to their terms, were evaluated at 4,100 pounds apiece, and a Negro girl was said to be worth 5,500 pounds.

These great differences in valuation of Negro and white "servants" strongly suggest, as does the failure to indicate term of service for the Negroes, that the latter were slaves at least in regard to life-time service. Beyond a question, there was some service which these blacks were rendering which enhanced their value—a service, moreover, which was not or could not be exacted from the whites. Furthermore, a Maryland deed of 1649 adumbrated slave status not only of life-time term, but of inheritance of status. Three Negroes "and all their issue both male and female" were deeded.

Russell and Ames culled from the Virginia court records of the 1640's and 1650's several instances of Negroes held in a status that can be called true slavery. For example, in 1646 a Negro woman and a Negro boy were sold to Stephen Charlton to be of use to him and his "heyers etc. for ever". A Negro girl was sold in 1652 "with her Issue and produce . . . and their services forever". Two years later a Negro girl was sold to one Armsteadinger "and his heyers . . . forever with all her increase both male and female". For March 12, 1655 the minutes of the Council and General Court of Virginia contain the entry, "Mulatto held to be a slave and appeal taken". Yet this is five years before Negro slavery is even implied in the statutes and fifteen before it is declared. An early case of what appears to be true slavery was found by Miss Ames on the Virginia eastern shore. In 1635 two Negroes were brought to the area; over twenty years later, in 1656, the widow of the master was bequeathing the child of one of the original Negroes and the other Negro and her children. This was much more than mere servitude—the term was longer than twenty years and apparently the status was inheritable.

Wesley Frank Craven, in his study of the seventeenth-century Southern colonies, has concluded that in the treatment of the Negro "the trend from the first was toward a sharp distinction between him and the white servant". In view of the evidence presented here, this seems a reasonable conclusion.

Concurrently with these examples of onerous service or actual slavery of Negroes, there were of course other members of the race who did gain their freedom. But the presence of Negroes rising out of servitude to freedom does not destroy the evidence that others were sinking into slavery; it merely underscores the unsteady evolution of a slave status. The supposition that the practice of slavery long antedated the law is strengthened by the tangential manner in which recognition of Negro slavery first appeared in the Virginia statutes. It occurred in 1660 in a law dealing with punishments for runaway servants, where casual reference was made to those "negroes who are incapable of making satisfaction by addition of time", since they were already serving for life.

Soon thereafter, as various legal questions regarding the status of Negroes came to the fore, the institution was further defined by statute law. In 1662 Virginia provided that the status of the offspring of a white man and a Negro would follow that of the mother—an interesting and unexplained departure from the common law and a reversion to Roman law. The same law stated that "any christian" fornicating "with a negro man or woman . . . shall pay double the fines imposed by the former act". Two years later Maryland prescribed service for Negroes "durante vita" and provided for hereditary status to descend through the father. Any free white woman who married a slave was to serve her husband's master for the duration of the slave's life, and her children would serve the master until they were thirty years of age. Presumably, no penalty was to be exacted of a free white man who married a Negro slave.

As early as 1669 the Virginia law virtually washed its hands of protecting the Negro held as a slave. It allowed punishment of refractory slaves up to and including accidental death, relieving the master, explicitly, of any fear of prosecution, on the assumption that no man would "destroy his owne estate".

In fact by 1680 the law of Virginia had erected a high wall around the Negro. One discerns in the phrase "any negro or other slave" how the word "negro" had taken on the meaning of slave. Moreover, in the act of 1680 one begins to see the lineaments of the later slave codes. No Negro may carry any weapon of any kind, nor leave his master's grounds without a pass, nor shall "any negroe or other slave . . . presume to lift his hand in opposition against any christian", and if a Negro runs away and resists recapture it "shalbe lawful for such person or persons to kill said negroe or slave . . .".

Yet it would be a quarter of a century before Negroes would comprise even a fifth of the population of Virginia. Thus long before slavery or black labor became an important part of the Southern economy, a special and inferior status had been worked out for the Negroes who came to the English colonies. Unquestionably it was a demand for labor which dragged the Negro to American shores, but the status which he acquired here cannot be explained by reference to that economic motive. Long before black labor was as economically important as unfree white labor, the Negro had been consigned to a special discriminatory status which mirrored the social discrimination Englishmen practised against him.

three
mutual causation
of the afro-american
condition

WINTHROP D. JORDAN

Born and raised in Massachusetts, Winthrop D. Jordan (b.1931)
received his undergraduate training at Harvard and his doctorate from
Brown (1960). He was a fellow at the Institute of Early American
History and Culture at Williamsburg, Virginia, during 1961–1963.
Professor of history at the University of California at Berkeley, Jordan
is best known for his book White over Black *on the origins of slavery*
in Anglo-America. This highly esteemed study is a comparative
analysis of the emergence of chattel slavery in the English mainland
colonies, and it reveals the interaction between attitudes and institutions
which defined the black man's role. Jordan contends that the first Negro
slaves were greeted by predetermined attitudes based upon tradition,
religion, and early European contacts with Africans.

Thanks to John Smith we know that Negroes first came to the
British continental colonies in 1619. What we do not know is
exactly when Negroes were first enslaved there. This question
has been debated by historians for the past seventy years, the
critical point being whether Negroes were enslaved almost from
their first importation or whether they were at first simply
servants and only later reduced to the status of slaves. The long
duration and vigor of the controversy suggest that more than a

Source: Winthrop D. Jordan, "Modern Tensions and the Origins of American
Slavery," *Journal of Southern History* 27 (February 1962): 18–30. Copyright ©
1962, Southern Historical Association. Reprinted by permission of the Managing
Editor. A modified and much more complete description of the origin of
American slavery is in Winthrop D. Jordan, *White over Black: American Attitudes*
toward the Negro 1550–1812 (Chapel Hill, 1968).

simple question of dating has been involved. In fact certain current tensions
in American society have complicated the historical problem and greatly heightened
its significance. Dating the origins of slavery has taken on a striking modern
relevance.

During the nineteenth century historians assumed almost universally that the first
Negroes came to Virginia as slaves. So close was their acquaintance with the problem of
racial slavery that it did not occur to them that Negroes could ever have been anything
but slaves. Philip A. Bruce, the first man to probe with some thoroughness into the
early years of American slavery, adopted this view in 1896, although he emphasized that
the original difference in treatment between white servants and Negroes was merely
that Negroes served for life. Just six years later, however, came a challenge from a
younger, professionally trained historian, James C. Ballagh. His *A History of Slavery in
Virginia* appeared in the *Johns Hopkins University Studies in Historical and Political Science,*
an aptly named series which was to usher in the new era of scholarly detachment in the
writing of institutional history. Ballagh offered a new and different interpretation; he
took the position that the first Negroes served merely as servants and that enslavement
did not begin until around 1660, when statutes bearing on slavery were passed for the
first time.

There has since been agreement on dating the statutory establishment of slavery, and
differences of opinion have centered on when enslavement began in actual practice.
Fortunately there has also been general agreement on slavery's distinguishing
characteristics: service for life and inheritance of like obligation by any offspring.
Writing on the free Negro in Virginia for the Johns Hopkins series, John H. Russell in
1913 tackled the central question and showed that some Negroes were indeed servants
but concluded that "between 1640 and 1660 slavery was fast becoming an established
fact. In this twenty years the colored population was divided, part being servants and
part being slaves, and some who were servants defended themselves with increasing
difficulty from the encroachments of slavery." Ulrich B. Phillips, though little
interested in the matter, in 1918 accepted Russell's conclusion of early servitude and
transition toward slavery after 1640. Helen T. Catterall took much the same position in
1926. On the other hand, in 1921 James M. Wright, discussing the free Negro in
Maryland, implied that Negroes were slaves almost from the beginning, and in 1940
Susie M. Ames reviewed several cases in Virginia which seemed to indicate that genuine
slavery had existed well before Ballagh's date of 1660.

All this was a very small academic gale, well insulated from the outside world. Yet
despite disagreement on dating enslavement, the earlier writers—Bruce, Ballagh, and
Russell—shared a common assumption which, though at the time seemingly irrelevant
to the main question, has since proved of considerable importance. They assumed that
prejudice against the Negro was natural and almost innate in the white man. It would
be surprising if they had felt otherwise in this period of segregation statutes, overseas
imperialism, immigration restriction, and full-throated Anglo-Saxonism. By the 1920's,
however, with the easing of these tensions, the assumption of natural prejudice was
dropped unnoticed. Yet only one historian explicitly contradicted that assumption:
Ulrich Phillips of Georgia, impressed with the geniality of both slavery and
twentieth-century race relations, found no natural prejudice in the white man and

expressed his "conviction that Southern racial asperities are mainly superficial, and that the two great elements are fundamentally in accord."

Only when tensions over race relations intensified once more did the older assumption of natural prejudice crop up again. After World War II American Negroes found themselves beneficiaries of New Deal politics and reforms, wartime need for manpower, world-wide repulsion at racist excesses in Nazi Germany, and growingly successful colored anticolonialism. With new militancy Negroes mounted an attack on the citadel of separate but equal, and soon it became clear that America was in for a period of self-conscious reappraisal of its racial arrangements. Writing in this period of heightened tension (1949) a practiced and careful scholar, Wesley F. Craven, raised the old question of the Negro's original status, suggesting that Negroes had been enslaved at an early date. Craven also cautiously resuscitated the idea that white men may have had natural distaste for the Negro, an idea which fitted neatly with the suggestion of early enslavement. Original antipathy would mean rapid debasement.

In the next year (1950) came a sophisticated counterstatement, which contradicted both Craven's dating and implicitly any suggestion of early prejudice. Oscar and Mary F. Handlin in "Origins of the Southern Labor System" offered a case for late enslavement, with servitude as the status of Negroes before about 1660. Originally the status of both Negroes and white servants was far short of freedom, the Handlins maintained, but Negroes failed to benefit from increased freedom for servants in mid-century and became less free rather than more. Embedded in this description of diverging status were broader implications: late and gradual enslavement undercut the possibility of natural, deep-seated antipathy toward Negroes. On the contrary, if whites and Negroes could share the same status of half freedom for forty years in the seventeenth century, why could they not share full freedom in the twentieth?

The same implications were rendered more explicit by Kenneth M. Stampp in a major reassessment of Southern slavery published two years after the Supreme Court's 1954 school decision. Reading physiology with the eye of faith, Stampp frankly stated his assumption "that innately Negroes *are,* after all, only white men with black skins, nothing more, nothing less." Closely following the Handlins' article on the origins of slavery itself, he almost directly denied any pattern of early and inherent racial antipathy: ". . . Negro and white servants of the seventeenth century seemed to be remarkably unconcerned about their visible physical differences." As for "the trend toward special treatment" of the Negro, "physical and cultural differences provided handy excuses to justify it." Distaste for the Negro, then, was in the beginning scarcely more than an appurtenance of slavery.

These views squared nicely with the hopes of those even more directly concerned with the problem of contemporary race relations, sociologists and social psychologists. Liberal on the race question almost to a man, they tended to see slavery as the initial cause of the Negro's current degradation. The modern Negro was the unhappy victim of long association with base status. Sociologists, though uninterested in tired questions of historical evidence, could not easily assume a natural prejudice in the white man as the cause of slavery. Natural or innate prejudice would not only violate their basic assumptions concerning the dominance of culture but would undermine the power of their new Baconian science. For if prejudice was natural there would be little one could do to wipe it out. Prejudice must have followed enslavement, not vice versa, else any liberal program of action would be badly compromised. One prominent social scientist suggested in a UNESCO pamphlet that racial prejudice in the United States commenced with the cotton gin!

Just how closely the question of dating had become tied to the practical matter of action against racial prejudice was made apparent by the suggestions of still another historian. Carl N. Degler grappled with the dating problem in an article frankly entitled "Slavery and the Genesis of American Race Prejudice." The article appeared in 1959, a time when Southern resistance to school desegregation seemed more adamant than ever and the North's hands none too clean, a period of discouragement for those hoping to end racial discrimination. Prejudice against the Negro now appeared firm and deep-seated, less easily eradicated than had been supposed in, say, 1954. It was Degler's view that enslavement began early, as a result of white settlers' prejudice or antipathy toward the first Negroes. Thus not only were the sociologists contradicted but the dating problem was now overtly and consciously tied to the broader question of whether slavery caused prejudice or prejudice caused slavery. A new self-consciousness over the American racial dilemma had snatched an arid historical controversy from the hands of an unsuspecting earlier generation and had tossed it into the arena of current debate.

Ironically there might have been no historical controversy at all if every historian dealing with the subject had exercised greater care with facts and greater restraint in interpretation. Too often the debate entered the realm of inference and assumption. For the crucial early years after 1619 there is simply not enough evidence to indicate with any certainty whether Negroes were treated like white servants or not. No historian has found anything resembling proof one way or the other. The first Negroes were sold to the English settlers, yet so were other Englishmen. It can be said, however, that Negroes were set apart from white men by the word *Negroes*, and a distinct name is not attached to a group unless it is seen as different. The earliest Virginia census reports plainly distinguished Negroes from white men, sometimes giving Negroes no personal name; and in 1629 every commander of the several plantations was ordered to "take a generall muster of all the inhabitants men woemen and Children as well *Englishe* as Negroes." Difference, however, might or might not involve inferiority.

The first evidence as to the actual status of Negroes does not appear until about 1640. Then it becomes clear that *some* Negroes were serving for life and some children inheriting the same obligation. Here it is necessary to suggest with some candor that the Handlins' statement to the contrary rests on unsatisfactory documentation. That some Negroes were held as slaves after about 1640 is no indication, however, that American slavery popped into the world fully developed at that time. Many historians, most cogently the Handlins, have shown slavery to have been a gradual development, a process not completed until the eighteenth century. The complete deprivation of civil and personal rights, the legal conversion of the Negro into a chattel, in short slavery as Americans came to know it, was not accomplished overnight. Yet these developments practically and logically depended on the practice of hereditary lifetime service, and it is certainly possible to find in the 1640's and 1650's traces of slavery's most essential feature.

The first definite trace appears in 1640 when the Virginia General Court pronounced sentence on three servants who had been retaken after running away to Maryland. Two of them, a Dutchman and a Scot, were ordered to serve their masters for one additional year and then the colony for three more, but "the third being a negro named John Punch shall serve his said master or his assigns for the time of his natural life here or else where." No white servant in America, so far as is known, ever received a like sentence. Later the same month a Negro was again singled out from a group of recaptured runaways; six of the seven were assigned additional time while the Negro was given none, presumably because he was already serving for life. After 1640, too, county court records began to mention Negroes, in part because there were more of them than previously—about two per cent of the Virginia population in 1649. Sales for life, often including any future progeny, were recorded in unmistakable language. In 1646 Francis Pott sold a Negro woman and boy to Stephen Charlton "to the use of him . . . forever." Similarly, six years later William Whittington sold to John Pott "one Negro girle named Jowan; aged about Ten yeares and with her Issue and produce duringe her (or either of them) for their Life tyme. And their Successors forever"; and a Maryland man in 1649 deeded two Negro men and a woman "and all their issue both male and Female." The executors of a York County estate in 1647 disposed of eight Negroes—four men, two women, and two children—to Captain John Chisman "to have hold occupy posesse and inioy and every one of the afforementioned Negroes forever[.]" The will of Rowland Burnham of "Rapahanocke," made in 1657, dispensed his considerable number of Negroes and white servants in language which clearly differentiated between the two by specifying that the whites were to serve for their "full terme of tyme" and the Negroes "for ever." Nor did anything in the will indicate that this distinction was exceptional or novel.

In addition to these clear indications that some Negroes were owned for life, there were cases of Negroes held for terms far longer than the normal five or seven years. On the other hand, some Negroes served only the term usual for white servants, and others were completely free. One Negro freeman, Anthony Johnson, himself owned a Negro. Obviously the enslavement of some Negroes did not mean the immediate enslavement of all.

Further evidence of Negroes serving for life lies in the prices paid for them. In many instances the valuations placed on Negroes (in estate inventories and bills of sale) were far higher than for white servants, even those servants with full terms yet to serve. Since there was ordinarily no preference for Negroes as such, higher prices must have meant that Negroes were more highly valued because of their greater length of service. Negro women may have been especially prized, moreover, because their progeny could also be held perpetually. In 1645, for example, two Negro women and a boy were sold for 5,500 pounds of tobacco. Two years earlier William Burdett's inventory listed eight servants (with the time each had still to serve) at valuations ranging from 400 to 1,100 pounds, while a "very anntient" Negro was valued at 3,000 and an eight-year-old Negro girl at 2,000 pounds, with no time-remaining indicated for either. In the late 1650's an inventory of Thomas Ludlow's large estate evaluated a white servant with six years to serve at less than an elderly Negro man and only one half of a Negro woman. The labor owned by James Stone in 1648 was evaluated as follows:

	lb tobo
Thomas Groves, 4 yeares to serve	1300
Francis Bomley for 6 yeares	1500
John Thackstone for 3 yeares	1300
Susan Davis for 3 yeares	1000
Emaniell a Negro man	2000
Roger Stone 3 yeares	1300
Mingo a Negro man	2000

Besides setting a higher value on the two Negroes, Stone's inventory, like Burdett's, failed to indicate the number of years they had still to serve. It would seem safe to assume that the time remaining was omitted in this and similar documents simply because the Negroes were regarded as serving for an unlimited time.

The situation in Maryland was apparently the same. In 1643 Governor Leonard Calvert agreed with John Skinner, "mariner," to exchange certain estates for seventeen sound Negro "slaves," fourteen men and three women between sixteen and twenty-six years old. The total value of these was placed at 24,000 pounds of tobacco, which would work out to 1,000 pounds for the women and 1,500 for the men, prices considerably higher than those paid for white servants at the time.

Wherever Negro women were involved, however, higher valuations may have reflected the fact that they could be used for field work while white women generally were not. This discrimination between Negro and white women, of course, fell short of actual enslavement. It meant merely that Negroes were set apart in a way clearly not to their advantage. Yet this is not the only evidence that Negroes were subjected to degrading distinctions not directly related to slavery. In several ways Negroes were singled out for special treatment which suggested a generalized debasing of Negroes as a group. Significantly, the first indications of debasement appeared at about the same time as the first indications of actual enslavement.

The distinction concerning field work is a case in point. It first appeared on the written record in 1643, when Virginia pointedly recognized it in her taxation policy. Previously tithable persons had been defined (1629) as "all those that worke in the ground of what qualitie or condition soever." Now the law stated that all adult men and *Negro* women were to be tithable, and this distinction was made twice again before 1660. Maryland followed a similar course, beginning in 1654. John Hammond, in a 1656 tract defending the tobacco colonies, wrote that servant women were not put to work in the fields but in domestic employments, "yet som wenches that are nasty, and beastly and not fit to be so imployed are put into the ground." Since all Negro women were taxed as working in the fields, it would seem logical to conclude that Virginians found them "nasty" and "beastly." The essentially racial nature of this discrimination was bared by a 1668 law at the time slavery was crystallizing on the statute books:

> *Whereas some doubts, have arisen whether negro women set free were still to be accompted tithable according to a former act, It is declared by this grand assembly that negro women, though permitted to enjoy their ffreedome yet ought not in all*

*respects to be admitted to a full fruition of the exemptions and impunities of the
English, and are still lyable to payment of taxes.*

Virginia law set Negroes apart in a second way by denying them the important right
and obligation to bear arms. Few restraints could indicate more clearly the denial to
Negroes of membership in the white community. This action, in a sense the first
foreshadowing of the slave codes, came in 1640, at just the time when other indications
first appear that Negroes were subject to special treatment.

Finally, an even more compelling sense of the separateness of Negroes was revealed
in early distress concerning sexual union between the races. In 1630 a Virginia court
pronounced a now famous sentence: "Hugh Davis to be soundly whipped, before an
assembly of Negroes and others for abusing himself to the dishonor of God and shame
of Christians, by defiling his body in lying with a negro." While there were other
instances of punishment for interracial union in the ensuing years, fornication rather
than miscegenation may well have been the primary offense, though in 1651 a Maryland
man sued someone who he claimed had said "that he had a black bastard in Virginia."
There may have been nothing racial about the 1640 case by which Robert Sweet was
compelled "to do penance in church according to laws of England, for getting a negroe
woman with child and the woman whipt." About 1650 a white man and a Negro
woman were required to stand clad in white sheets before a congregation in Lower
Norfolk County for having had relations, but this punishment was sometimes used in
ordinary cases of fornication between two whites.

It is certain, however, that in the early 1660's when slavery was gaining statutory
recognition, the colonial assemblies legislated with feeling against miscegenation. Nor
was this merely a matter of avoiding confusion of status, as was suggested by the
Handlins. In 1662 Virginia declared that "if any christian shall committ ffornication
with a negro man or woman, hee or shee soe offending" should pay double the usual
fine. Two years later Maryland prohibited interracial marriages:

*. . . forasmuch as divers freeborne English women forgettfull of their free Condicōn
and to the disgrace of our Nation doe intermarry with Negro Slaves by which alsoe
divers suites may arise touching the Issue of such woemen and a great damage doth
befall the Masters of such Negroes for prevention whereof for deterring such freeborne
women from such shameful Matches. . . .*

Strong language indeed if the problem had only been confusion of status. A Maryland
act of 1681 described marriages of white women with Negroes as, among other things,
"always to the Satisfaccōn of theire Lascivious & Lustfull desires, & to the disgrace not
only of the English butt allso of many other Christian Nations." When Virginia finally
prohibited all interracial liaisons in 1691, the assembly vigorously denounced
miscegenation and its fruits as "that abominable mixture and spurious issue."

One is confronted, then, with the fact that the first evidences of enslavement and of
other forms of debasement appeared at about the same time. Such coincidence comports
poorly with both views on the causation of prejudice and slavery. If slavery caused
prejudice, then invidious distinctions concerning working in the fields, bearing arms,

and sexual union should have appeared only after slavery's firm establishment. If prejudice caused slavery, then one would expect to find such lesser discriminations preceding the greater discrimination of outright enslavement.

Perhaps a third explanation of the relationship between slavery and prejudice may be offered, one that might fit the pattern of events as revealed by existing evidence. Both current views share a common starting point: They predicate two factors, prejudice and slavery, and demand a distinct order of causality. No matter how qualified by recognition that the effect may in turn react upon the cause, each approach inevitably tends to deny the validity of its opposite. But what if one were to regard both slavery and prejudice as species of a general debasement of the Negro? Both may have been equally cause and effect, constantly reacting upon each other, dynamically joining hands to hustle the Negro down the road to complete degradation. Mutual causation is, of course, a highly useful concept for describing social situations in the modern world. Indeed it has been widely applied in only slightly altered fashion to the current racial situation: Racial prejudice and the Negro's lowly position are widely accepted as constantly reinforcing each other.

This way of looking at the facts might well fit better with what we know of slavery itself. Slavery was an organized pattern of human relationships. No matter what the law might say, it was of different character than cattle ownership. No matter how degrading, slavery involved human beings. No one seriously pretended otherwise. Slavery was not an isolated economic or institutional phenomenon; it was the practical facet of a general debasement without which slavery could have no rationality. (Prejudice, too, was a form of debasement, a kind of slavery in the mind.) Certainly the urgent need for labor in a virgin country guided the direction which debasement took, molded it, in fact, into an institutional framework. That economic practicalities shaped the external form of debasement should not tempt one to forget, however, that slavery was at bottom a social arrangement, a way of society's ordering its members in its own mind.

part two
the
classic
statements

four
slavery: a wrong
to the slave

JAMES FORD RHODES

The sectional animosities that influenced much of the writing on slavery
before and after the Civil War were forsworn by James Ford Rhodes
(1848–1927) in his multivolume History of the United States from
the Compromise of 1850. *The northern-born Rhodes, who turned to*
the writing of history after a successful career in business, sought to be
fair-minded in his appraisal of the South's "peculiar institution."
Rhodes did find a few kind slaveholders, and he admitted that
abolitionists exaggerated the evils of bondage; but he found virtually no
redeeming qualities in the treatment meted out to the slaves who were
poorly fed, clothed and housed, and "always worked under the lash."

It was the cultivation of the semi-tropical products, cotton, sugar,
and rice, that strengthened the hold of slavery on the South. No
one was able to contend, with any success, that grain and tobacco
could be as well cultivated by slave as by free labor. After a very
careful investigation into the agricultural system of Virginia,
Olmsted, who worked a farm in New York, arrived at the
conclusion that one hand in New York did as much labor as two
slave hands in Virginia. Yet taking as a basis the price paid for
slaves when they were hired out—a common custom in Eastern
Virginia—he was well satisfied that the wages for common
laborers were twenty-five per cent higher in Virginia than in
New York. What was true of Virginia was substantially true of
the other border slave States. It should have been clear that, in
the portion of the South where the climate was unsuitable for
cotton-raising, slavery was an economical failure; and before the
war, as at present, this conclusion necessarily followed the

Source: James Ford Rhodes, *History of the United States from the Compromise of*
1850, Vol. I (New York: Macmillan, 1893), pp. 303–19, 323–28.

inquiries of an impartial observer. If there had been any justification for slavery it must have been found in the cotton, rice, and sugar regions.

What was there in mitigation of the wrong done the slave? It used to be said that the slaves were better fed, better clothed, and better lodged than laborers in the cites and manufacturing districts at the North. Yet no statement more completely false was ever made. A report to the Secretary of the Treasury from forty-six sugar-planters of Louisiana stated that the cost of feeding and clothing an able-bodied slave was thirty dollars per year. Olmsted estimates that the clothing would amount to ten dollars, which would leave twenty dollars for the food, or five and one half cents per day. "Does the food of a first-rate laborer," he asks, "anywhere in the free world cost less?" This was a fair example of the cost of supporting the negroes on the large sugar and cotton plantations of the Southwest. Corn-meal was the invariable article of food furnished the slaves; bacon and molasses were regularly provided on some plantations, while on others they were only occasional luxuries. Fanny Kemble, the accomplished actress, who spent a winter on her husband's rice and cotton plantations in Georgia, says that animal food was only given to men who were engaged in the hardest kind of work, such as ditching, and to them it was given only occasionally and in moderate quantities. Her description of the little negroes begging her piteously for meat is as pathetic as the incident of the hungry demand of Oliver Twist. This rude fare was generally given the slave in sufficient quantity; the instances are rare in which one finds the negroes did not have enough to eat. Frederick Douglass, however, tells us that, when a child, although belonging to a wealthy and large landed proprietor of Maryland, he was often pinched with hunger, and used to dispute with the dogs the crumbs which fell from the kitchen table. In comparison with slaves who had plenty, the prison convicts of the North were given food in greater variety and not so coarse. "Ninety-nine in a hundred of our free laborers," wrote Olmsted, "from choice and not from necessity, live, in respect to food, at least four times as well as the average of the hardest-worked slaves on the Louisiana sugar plantations." The negroes on the large cotton plantations of the Southwest fared no better. A Louisiana cotton-planter furnished De Bow an itemized estimate of the cost of raising cotton, in which the expense of feeding one hundred slaves, furnishing the hospital, overseer's table, etc., was put down at $750 for the year. This was $7.50 for each one, or, in other words, the cost of food for the slave was less than $2\frac{1}{12}$ cents per day. The overseers everywhere endeavored to bring the keeping of the slaves down to the lowest possible figure. This was a large item in the cost of cotton production; and on the large plantations, where in some cases as many as five hundred slaves were worked, economy in feeding these human cattle was studied with almost scientific precision. The supply of food to the slaves was made a subject of legislation. Louisiana required that meat should be furnished, but this law became a dead letter. North Carolina fixed the daily allowance of corn; in the other States the law was not specific, but directed in general terms that the provisions should be sufficient for the health of the slave.

It was in the line of plantation parsimony that the clothes furnished the field hands should be of the cheapest material and as scant as was consistent with a slight regard for decency and health. All observers agree that the slaves who labored on the cotton and sugar plantations presented a ragged, unkempt, and dirty appearance.

Comfortable houses were in many places built for the negroes; but, owing to their indolent and filthy habits, which were aggravated by their condition of servitude, neatness and the appearance of comfort soon disappeared from their quarters. The testimony is almost universal that the negro cabins were foul and wretched.

In the cotton, sugar, and rice districts the negroes were hard worked. The legal limit of a day's work in South Carolina was fifteen hours; on cotton plantations, during the picking season, the slaves labored sixteen hours, while on sugar plantations at grinding time eighteen hours' work was exacted. Many of the large owners of land and of negroes in the Southwest were absentees, whose authority was delegated to their overseers. Indeed, in all cases where the agricultural operations were on a large scale, the overseer was the power. Patrick Henry described the overseers as "the most abject, degraded, unprincipled race." Years had not improved them, and on the lonely plantations of the Southwest they were hardly amenable to public opinion or subject to the law's control. They were generally ignorant, frequently intemperate, always despotic and brutal. Their value was rated according to the bigness of the cotton crop they made, and, with that end in view, they spared not the slave. The slaves always worked under the lash. "It is true," said Chancellor Harper, in his defence of slavery, "that the slave is driven to labor by stripes." With each gang went a stout negro driver whose qualification for the position depended upon his unusual cruelty; he followed the working slaves, urging them in their task by a loud voice and the cracking of his long whip. That the negroes were overtasked to the extent of being often permanently injured, was evident from the complaints made by the Southern agricultural journals against the bad policy of thus wasting human property. An Alabama tradesman told Olmsted that if the overseers make "plenty of cotton, the owners never ask how many niggers they kill;" and he gave the further information that a determined and perfectly relentless overseer could get almost any wages he demanded, for when it became known that such a man had made so many bales to the hand, everybody would try to get him.

In the rich cotton-planting districts the negro was universally regarded as property. When the newspapers mentioned the sudden death of one of them, it was the loss of money that was bewailed, and not of the light which no Promethean heat can relume. Olmsted found that "negro life and negro vigor were generally much less carefully economized than I had always before imagined them to be." Louisiana sugar-planters did not hesitate to avow openly that, on the whole, they found it the best economy to work off their stock of negroes about once in seven years, and then buy an entire set of new hands. An overseer once said to Olmsted: "Why, sir, I wouldn't mind killing a nigger more than I would a dog." The restraint of the law did not operate powerfully to prevent the killing of these unfortunates. While the wilful, malicious, and premeditated murder of a slave was a capital offence in all the slave-holding States, it was provided in most of them that any person killing a slave in the act of resistance to his lawful owner was guilty of no offence, nor was there ground for an indictment in the case where a slave died while receiving moderate correction. But what protected the overseers on plantations remote from settlements and neighbors was the universal rule of slave law, that the testimony of a colored person could not be received against a white. This gave complete immunity to the despotic overseer. On but few plantations were there more than two white men, and they were always interested parties, being owner, manager, or overseer. As a matter of fact, only refractory slaves, or negroes attempting to run away, were killed, and these murders were not frequent. Except in rare instances the slaves had no incentive to work, save the fear of a whipping. "If you don't work faster," or "if you don't work better, I will have you flogged," were words often heard. No one can wonder that it was a painful sight to see negroes at work. The besotted and generally repulsive expression of the field hands; their brute-like countenances, on which were painted stupidity, indolence, duplicity, and sensuality; their listlessness; their dogged action; the stupid, plodding, machine-like manner in which they labored, made a sorrowful picture of man's inhumanity to man. General Sherman, who was for a time stationed at New Orleans and later lived more than a year in Louisiana, states that the field slaves were treated like animals. Fanny Kemble noticed that those who had some intelligence, who were beyond the brutish level, wore a pathetic expression—a mixture of sadness and fear. Frederick Douglass, himself a slave and the only negro in his neighborhood who could read, relates the effect of unceasing and habitual toil on one in whom there was a gleam of knowledge: "My natural elasticity was crushed; my intellect languished; the disposition to read departed; the cheerful spark that lingered about my eye died out; the dark night of slavery closed in upon me, and behold a man transformed to a brute." An observer who visited an average rice plantation near Savannah was impressed with the fate of the field hands: "Their lot was one of continued toil from morning to night, uncheered even by the hope of any change or prospect of improvement in condition." Harriet Martineau wrote: "A walk through a lunatic asylum is far less painful than a visit to the slave quarter of an estate." This state of affairs is perfectly comprehensible; it was an accessory of the system. It was Olmsted's judgment that a certain degree of cruelty was necessary to make slave labor generally profitable.

The institution bore harder on the women than on the men. Slave-breeding formed an important part of plantation economy, being encouraged as was the breeding of animals. "Their lives are, for the most part, those of mere animals;" wrote Fanny Kemble, "their increase is literally mere animal breeding, to which every encouragement is given, for it adds to the master's live-stock and the value of his estate." The women worked in the fields as did the men. When it became known that they were pregnant, their task was lightened, yet, if necessary, they were whipped when with child, and, in some cases, were put to work again as early as three weeks after their confinement, although generally the time of rest allowed was one month. Fanny Kemble's woman heart bled at the tales of suffering she heard, of the rapid child-bearing, the gross disregard of nature's laws of maternity, and the consequent wide prevalence of diseases peculiar to the sex; her daily record of what she saw and heard is as pitiful as it is true. . . .

Slaves were chattels. They could be transferred by a simple bill of sale as horses or cattle; they could even be sold or given away by their masters without a writing. The cruelty of separating families, involved in the business of selling slaves who were raised expressly for market, or in the division of negroes among the heirs of a decedent, or in their forced sale occasioned by the bankruptcy of an owner, appealed very forcibly to the North. It especially awakened the sympathy of Northern women, who counted for much in educating and influencing voters in a way that finally brought about the aboliton of slavery. These separations were not infrequent, although they were not the general rule. There was a disposition, on the score of self-interest, to avoid the tearing asunder of family ties, for the reason that if slaves pined on account of parting from those to whom they had become attached, they labored less obediently and were more troublesome. Humane masters would, whenever possible, avoid selling the husband apart from the wife, or young children away from the mother. The best public sentiment of the South frowned upon an unnecessary separation of families. It was not unusual to find men making a money sacrifice to prevent a rending of family attachments, or generous people contributing a sum to avert such an evil. The prominence given in their arguments by the abolitionists to this feature of the system undoubtedly influenced the South to abate this cruelty. The apologists of slavery never defended the separation of families; it was admitted to be a necessary evil, and pains were taken to give Northern and foreign visitors the impression that such cases were of rare occurrence. . . .

It could not be denied that an extensive traffic in slaves existed all through the South. "Cash for Negroes," "Negroes for Sale," and "Negroes Wanted," were as common advertisements in the Southern papers as notices of proposed sales of horses and mules. Indeed, the two kinds of property were frequently advertised and sold together. An administrator offers "horses, mules, cattle, hogs, sheep, and several likely young negroes;" a sheriff announces the sale of "ten head of cattle, twenty-five head of hogs, and seven negroes;" an auctioneer bespeaks attendance at the courthouse in Columbia, S.C., for an opportunity such as seldom occurs, for he will offer one hundred valuable negroes, among whom are "twenty-five prime young men, forty of the most likely young women, and as fine a set of children as can be shown." A dealer at Memphis offers the highest cash price for slaves, and one at Baltimore wants to buy five thousand negroes and announces that families are "never separated." A firm at Natchez, Miss., advertises "fresh arrivals weekly of slaves," and promises to keep constantly "a large and well-selected stock." A competitor in the same city offers "ninety negroes just arrived from Richmond, consisting of field hands, house-servants, carriage-drivers, several fine cooks, and some excellent mules, and one very fine riding horse;" and he advises his patrons that he has "made arrangements in Richmond to have regular shipments every month, and intends to keep a good stock on hand of every description of servants." An auctioneer in New Orleans announces for sale three splendid paintings, "The Circassian Slave," "The Lion Fight," and "The Crucifixion;" also, "Delia, aged seventeen, a first-rate cook; Susan, aged sixteen, a mulatress, a good house-girl; Ben, aged fourteen, and Peyton, aged sixteen, smart house-boys;" and adds, "The above slaves are fully guaranteed and sold for no fault." A storekeeper of New Orleans, who was also a colonel, at the request of his many acquaintances, got up for their amusement a raffle where the prizes were a dark-bay horse, warranted sound, with a trotting buggy and harness, and "the stout mulatto girl Sarah, aged about twenty-nine years, general house-servant, valued at nine hundred dollars and guaranteed." There might be seen now and then in the New Orleans papers an advertisement of a lot of pious negroes. A curious notice appeared in the *Religious Herald*, a Baptist journal published in Richmond: "Who wants thirty-five thousand dollars in property? I am desirous to spend the balance of my life as a missionary, if the Lord permit, and therefore offer for sale my farm—the vineyard adjacent to Williamsburg . . . and also about forty servants, mostly young and likely, and rapidly increasing in numbers and value." By actual count made from the advertisements in sixty-four newspapers published in eight slave States during the last two weeks of November, 1852, there were offered for sale four thousand one hundred negroes. The good society of the South looked upon slave dealers and auctioneers with contempt. Their occupation was regarded as base, and they were treated by gentlemen as the publicans were by the Pharisees. The opening scene of "Uncle Tom's Cabin" was criticised as inaccurate, for it showed a Kentucky gentleman entertaining at table a vulgar slave-dealer. The utter scorn with which such men were regarded was a condemnation of slavery in the house of its friends.

A feature of the institution that aroused much indignation at the North was its cruelty, as evidenced by the rigor with which the lash was used. We have seen that flogging necessarily accompanied this system of labor. The master and the overseer held the theory that the negroes were but children and should be chastised on the principle of the ancient schoolmaster who carried out the injunctions of Solomon. This was also in the main the practice, but wanton cruelty did not rule. At times, however, a fit of drunkenness, an access of ill-temper, or a burst of passion would incite the man who had unrestrained power to use it like a brute. Abolition literature is full of such instances, well attested.

Slaves were sometimes whipped to death. The murderers were occasionally tried, and once in a while convicted, but they were never hanged; more frequently, however, as the violent act was usually witnessed only by negroes, no proof could be obtained, and the perpetrator was not even arrested. When negroes themselves committed a capital crime, there were instances of burning them to death at the stake.

One finds, however, notice of plantations on which the slaves were never whipped. Ampère, who had no sympathy with slavery, visited a German who owned a plantation near Charleston, and who, having no cruelty or tyranny in his nature, appeared to be literally oppressed by his blacks. He was so humane that he would not whip his slaves. The slaves showed him little gratitude, and labored sluggishly and with great carelessness. When he went into a cabin where the negresses were at work cleaning cotton, he confined himself to showing them how badly their task was done and explaining to them the considerable damage which their negligence caused him. His observations were received with grumbling and sullenness. Ampère saw in this case an excellent argument against slavery. Had the gentleman hired his laborers he would have dismissed them if they did not work to his liking; but under the Southern system his choice lay simply between whipping them or becoming a victim to their idleness. Masters like this were certainly rare in the cotton region, but as one travelled northward, slavery appeared under milder features. A New England girl became a governess upon a Tennessee plantation where no slave had been whipped for seven years; she became reconciled to slavery, and did not find in reality the "revolting horrors" in it for which a Northern education had prepared her. In Virginia, Olmsted saw no whipping of slaves except of wild, lazy children as they were being broken in to work; and he heard of but little harshness or cruelty.

In our time, when the desire for education is common to all, and the need of it universally acknowledged, it is interesting to inquire how this matter was dealt with by the slave-holders. North Carolina, South Carolina, Georgia, Alabama, and Louisiana forbade, under penalties, the teaching of slaves to read or write. In Virginia the owners, but no one else, might instruct their negroes, and in North Carolina the slaves might be taught arithmetic. Some of these enactments were on the statute-books before 1831, but everywhere after that date the laws were made more stringent and were more effectually enforced. This year was memorable for the Nat Turner insurrection and for the beginning of a systematic abolition agitation by Garrison in the *Liberator*. The usual apology at the South for these laws was their alleged necessity to prevent the negroes from reading the abolition documents sent to the slave States, which were incitements to insurrection. The course which legislation took after 1831 has led many Northern writers to infer that the anti-slavery agitation was the cause of slaves being treated more inhumanly than before. In so far as the withholding of privileges of education and association was a cruelty they are right; but they are wrong when they have assumed that more positive brutality prevailed. A careful examination of the slavery literature will hardly fail to lead to the conclusion that the flood of light which the abolitionists threw upon the practice influenced the slave-owners to mitigate its most cruel features. The thesis that slavery is a positive good began to be maintained after 1831, but no amount of arrogant assertion could prevent the advocates of slavery from being put on the defensive. Their earnest endeavors to convince Northern and foreign visitors of the benefits of the system show their appreciation of the fact that it was under the ban of the civilized world; and this very necessity of justifying their peculiar institution made them desirous of suppressing, as far as possible, those features of it which they admitted to be evil.

five
slavery: a school
for civilizing

ULRICH B. PHILLIPS

*Modern scholarship on slavery began with Ulrich Bonnell Phillips
(1877–1934), a Georgia-born historian who took his Ph.D. at
Columbia and spent most of his teaching career at northern universities.
Phillips was the first scholar investigating slavery to use extensively
original manuscript sources such as plantation account books. His
thoroughly researched works,* American Negro Slavery *(1918) and*
Life and Labor in the Old South *(1929), influenced a whole
generation of writers on the subject.*

The plantation force was a conscript army, living in barracks and
on constant "fatigue." Husbands and wives were comrades in
service under an authority as complete as the commanding
personnel could wish. The master was captain and quartermaster
combined, issuing orders and distributing rations. The overseer
and the foreman, where there were such, were lieutenant and
sergeant to see that orders were executed. The field hands were
privates with no choice but to obey unless, like other seasoned
soldiers, they could dodge the duties assigned.

But the plantation was also a homestead, isolated, permanent
and peopled by a social group with a common interest in
achieving and maintaining social order. Its régime was shaped by
the customary human forces, interchange of ideas and
coadaptation of conduct. The intermingling of white and black
children in their pastimes was no more continuous
or influential than the adult interplay of command

Source: Ulrich B. Phillips, *Life and Labor in the Old South* (Boston: Little, Brown,
1929), pp. 196–209. Copyright 1929 by Little, Brown and Company. Copyright
©, 1959 by Mrs. Ulrich B. Phillips. Copyright © 1963 by Little, Brown and
Company. Reprinted by permission of Little, Brown and Co.

and response, of protest and concession. In so far as harmony was attained—and in this the plantation mistress was a great if quiet factor—a common tradition was evolved embodying reciprocal patterns of conventional conduct.

The plantation was of course a factory, in which robust laborers were essential to profits. Its mere maintenance as a going concern required the proprietor to sustain the strength and safeguard the health of his operatives and of their children, who were also his, destined in time to take their parents' places. The basic food allowance came to be somewhat standardized at a quart of corn meal and half a pound of salt pork per day for each adult and proportionably for children, commuted or supplemented with sweet potatoes, field peas, sirup, rice, fruit and "garden sass" as locality and season might suggest. The clothing was coarse, and shoes were furnished only for winter. The housing was in huts of one or two rooms per family, commonly crude but weather-tight. Fuel was abundant. The sanitation of the clustered cabins was usually a matter of systematic attention; and medical service was at least commensurate with the groping science of the time and the sparse population of the country. Many of the larger plantations had central kitchens, day nurseries, infirmaries and physicians on contract for periodic visits. The aged and infirm must be cared for along with the young and able-bodied, to maintain the good will of their kinsmen among the workers, if for no other reason. Morale was no less needed than muscle if performance were to be kept above a barely tolerable minimum.

The plantation was a school. An intelligent master would consult his own interest by affording every talented slave special instruction and by inculcating into the commoner sort as much routine efficiency, regularity and responsibility as they would accept. Not only were many youths given training in the crafts, and many taught to read and write, even though the laws forbade it, but a goodly number of planters devised and applied plans to give their whole corps spontaneous incentive to relieve the need of detailed supervision. Thus John McDonogh near New Orleans instituted in 1825 an elaborate scheme of self-government and self-driving with a prospect of self-emancipation by his corps as a unit; and a plan of trial by a jury of his peers for any slave charged with a plantation offense was followed by Joseph and Jefferson Davis on "Hurricane" and "Briarfield" in Mississippi. The traveler Liancourt when visiting the Pringle plantation in the South Carolina lowlands in 1796 found its proprietor "in every respect a worthy man, amiable and communicative, and so happy that his equals are but seldom found. He is an excellent master to his Negroes, and asserts, against the opinion of many others, that the plantations of mild and indulgent masters thrive most and that the Negroes are most industrious and faithful. He is beloved by his slaves. The cultivated part of his plantation is in the best order, and the number of his slaves increases yearly by a tenth." A similar achievement was described to Frederika Bremer as that of Thomas Spalding of Sapelo on the Georgia coast, "a rich old gentleman who upon the beautiful island where he lives has allowed the palmettoes to grow in freedom, and the Negroes to live and work in freedom also, governed alone by the law of duty and love, and where all succeeds excellently." We share Miss Bremer's regret that she could not accept an invitation to visit this Elysium. We have, however, from the pen of William Faux a description of such an establishment in the Carolina uplands, that of the venerable Mr. Mickle, who said of his slaves: "They are all, old and young, true and faithful to my interests; they need no taskmaster, no overseer; they will do all and more than I expect them to do, and I can trust them with untold gold. . . . I respect them as my children, and they look on me as their friend and father." And the traveler says: "This conversation induced me to view more attentively the faces of the adult slaves; and I was astonished at the free, easy, sober, intelligent and thoughtful impression which such an economy as Mr. Mickle's had indelibly made on their countenances."

The civilizing of the Negroes was not merely a consequence of definite schooling but a fruit of plantation life itself. The white household taught perhaps less by precept than by example. It had much the effect of a "social settlement" in a modern city slum, furnishing models of speech and conduct, along with advice on occasion, which the vicinage is invited to accept. The successes of Pringle, Spalding and Mickle, if correctly reported, were quite extraordinary. Most planters did not even attempt an emulation, for not one in a hundred could hope by his own genius and magnetism to break the grip of normal slave-plantation circumstance. The bulk of the black personnel was notoriously primitive, uncouth, improvident and inconstant, merely because they were Negroes of the time; and by their slave status they were relieved from the pressure of want and debarred from any full-force incentive of gain.

Many planters, however, sought to promote contentment, loyalty and zeal by gifts and rewards, and by sanctioning the keeping of poultry and pigs and the cultivation of little fields in off times with the privilege of selling any produce. In the cotton belt the growing of nankeen cotton was particularly encouraged, for its brownish color would betray any surreptitious addition from the master's own fields. Some indeed had definite bonus systems. A. H. Bernard of Virginia determined at the close of 1836 to replace his overseer with a slave foreman, and announced to his Negroes that in case of good service by the corps he would thereafter distribute premiums to the amount of what had been the overseer's wages. After six months' trial he wrote: "I can say for this experiment that never certainly in my life have I had so much work so well done nor with equal cheerfulness and satisfaction, not having had occasion to utter an angry word except to a little cattle minder." And in Louisiana sundry planters made it a Christmas practice to distribute among the heads of industrious families a sum amounting in aggregate to a dollar for each hogshead of sugar in the year's product.

But any copious resort to profit-sharing schemes was avoided at large as being likely to cost more than it would yield in increment to the planter's own crop. The generality of planters, it would seem, considered it hopeless to make their field hands into thorough workmen or full-fledged men, and contented themselves with very moderate achievement. Tiring of endless correction and unfruitful exhortation, they relied somewhat supinely upon authority with a tone of kindly patronage and a baffled acquiescence in slack service.

For example a French traveler in South Carolina at the middle of the nineteenth century reported his observations on the plantation of a German, "certainly the least cruel and tyrannical of men, . . . who does not wish to beat his slaves. The ungrateful slaves work with great laziness and carelessness. When he entered a hut where the Negresses were cleaning cotton he was content to show them how badly it was done. . . . The result of his remarks was a pout and a little grumbling." And there was no sequel except a plea from the planter for the visitor's commiseration.

It has been said by a critic of the twentieth century South: "In some ways the negro is shamefully mistreated—mistreated through leniency," which permits him as a tenant or employee to lean upon the whites in a continuous mental siesta and sponge upon them habitually, instead of requiring him to stand upon his own moral and economic legs. The same censure would apply as truly in any preceding generation. The slave plantation, like other schools, was conditioned by the nature and habituations of its teachers and pupils. Its instruction was inevitably slow; and the effect of its discipline was restricted by the fact that even its aptest pupils had no diploma in prospect which would send them forth to fend for themselves.

The plantation was a parish, or perhaps a chapel of ease. Some planters assumed the functions of lay readers when ordained ministers were not available, or joined the congregation even when Negro preachers preached. Bishop Leonidas Polk was chief chaplain on his own estate, and is said to have suffered none of his slaves to be other than Episcopalian; but the generality of masters gave full freedom as to church connection.

The legislature of Barbados, when urged by the governor in 1681 to promote the Christianization of slaves on that island, replied, "their savage brutishness renders them wholly incapable. Many have endeavoured it without success." But on the continent such sentiments had small echo; and as decades passed masters and churches concerned themselves increasingly in the premises. A black preacher might meet rebuke and even run a risk of being lynched if he harped too loudly upon the liberation of the Hebrews from Egyptian bondage; but a moderate supervision would prevent such indiscretions. The Sermon on the Mount would be harmless despite its suggestion of an earthly inheritance for the meek; the Decalogue was utterly sound; and "servants obey your masters", "render unto Caesar the things that are Caesar's", and "well done, thou good and faithful servant" were invaluable texts for homilies. The Methodists and Baptists were inclined to invite ecstasy from free and slave alike. Episcopalians and Presbyterians, and the Catholics likewise, deprecating exuberance, dealt rather in quiet precept than in fervid exhortation—with far smaller statistical results.

The plantation was a pageant and a variety show in alternation. The procession of plowmen at evening, slouched crosswise on their mules; the dance in the new sugarhouse, preceded by prayer; the bonfire in the quarter with contests in clogs, cakewalks and Charlestons whose fascinations were as yet undiscovered by the great world; the work songs in solo and refrain, with not too fast a rhythm; the baptizing in the creek, with lively demonstrations from the "sisters" as they came dripping out; the torchlight pursuit of 'possum and 'coon, with full-voiced halloo to baying houn' dawg and yelping cur; the rabbit hunt, the log-rolling, the house-raising, the husking bee, the quilting party, the wedding, the cock fight, the crap game, the children's play, all punctuated plantation life—and most of them were highly vocal. A funeral now and then of some prominent slave would bring festive sorrowing, or the death of a beloved master an outburst of emotion.

The plantation was a matrimonial bureau, something of a harem perhaps, a copious nursery, and a divorce court. John Brickell wrote of colonial North Carolina: "It frequently happens, when these women have no Children by the first Husband, after being a year or two cohabiting together, the Planters oblige them to take a second, third, fourth, fifth, or more Husbands or Bedfellows; a fruitful Woman amongst them being very much valued by the Planters, and a numerous Issue esteemed the greatest Riches in this Country." By running on to five or more husbands for a constantly barren woman Brickell discredits his own statement. Yet it may have had a kernel of truth, and it is quite possible that something of such a policy persisted throughout the generations. These things do not readily get into the records. I have myself heard a stalwart Negro express a humorous regret that he was free, for said he in substance: "If I had lived in slavery times my master would have given me half a dozen wives and taken care of all the children." This may perhaps voice a tradition among slave descendants, and the tradition may in turn derive from an actual sanction of polygamy by some of the masters. A planter doubtless described a practice not unique when he said "that he interfered as little as possible with their domestic habits except in matters of police. 'We don't care what they do when their tasks are over—we lose sight of them till next day. Their morals and manners are in their own keeping. The men may have, for instance, as many wives as they please, so long as they do not quarrel about such matters.' " But another was surely no less representative when he instructed his overseer: "Marriages shall be performed in every instance of a nuptial contract, and the parties settled off to themselves without encumbering other houses to give discontent. No slave shall be allowed to cohabit with two or more wives or husbands at the same time; doing so shall subject them to a strict trial and severe punishment."

Life was without doubt monogamous in general; and some of the matings were by order, though the generality were pretty surely spontaneous. This item, written by an overseer to his employer, is typical of many: "Esaw and biner has asked permission to Marry. I think it a good Match. What say you to it?" Here and there a man had what was called in slave circles a "broad wife", a wife belonging to another master and dwelling at a distance. Planters of course preferred their slaves to be mated at home.

In the number of their children the Negro women rivaled the remarkable fecundity of their mistresses. One phenomenal slave mother bore forty-one children, mostly of course as twins; and the records of many others ran well above a dozen each. As a rule, perhaps, babies were even more welcome to slave women than to free; for childbearing brought lightened work during pregnancy and suckling, and a lack of ambition conspired with a freedom from economic anxiety to clear the path of maternal impulse.

Concubinage of Negro women to planters and their sons and overseers is evidenced by the census enumeration of mulattoes and by other data. It was flagrantly prevalent in the Creole section of Louisiana, and was at least sporadic from New England to Texas. The régime of slavery facilitated concubinage not merely by making black women subject to white men's wills but by promoting intimacy and weakening racial antipathy. The children, of whatever shade or paternity, were alike the property of the mother's owner and were nourished on the plantation. Not a few mulattoes, however, were manumitted by their fathers and vested with property.

Slave marriages, not being legal contracts, might be dissolved without recourse to public tribunals. Only the master's consent was required, and this was doubtless not hard to get. On one plantation systematic provision was made in the standing regulations: "When sufficient cause can be shewn on either side, a marriage may be annulled; but the offending party must be severely punished. Where both are in the wrong, both must be punished, and if they insist on separating must have a hundred lashes apiece. After such a separation, neither can marry again for three years." If such a system were in general effect in our time it would lessen the volume of divorce in American society. But it may be presumed that most plantation rules were not so stringent.

The home of a planter or of a well-to-do townsman was likely to be a "magnificent negro boarding-house", at which and from which an indefinite number of servants and their dependents and friends were fed. In town the tribe might increase to the point of embarrassment. A Savannah woman wrote: "My only reason for desiring a plantation at times is for my host of little and big people—few to be sure of the latter and quite too many of the former. The city, to my dear bought experience, is a bad place, though I have nothing to complain of with regard to the conduct of my people." The domestics were likely to consider themselves entitled to luxurious fare. The wife of a Congressman when visiting her home after two years' absence wrote: "I have been mobbed by my own house servants. . . . They agreed to come in a body and beg me to stay at home to keep my own house once more. . . . I asked my cook if she lacked anything on the plantation at the Hermitage. 'Lack anything?' she said, 'I lack everything, what are corn meal, bacon, milk and molasses? Would that be all you wanted? Ain't I been living and eating exactly as you all these years? When I cook for you, didn't I have some of all? Dere now!' Then she doubled herself up laughing. They all shouted, 'Missis, we is crazy for you to stay home.' "

Each plantation had a hierarchy. Not only were the master and his family exalted to a degree beyond the reach of slave aspiration, but among the Negroes themselves there were pronounced gradations of rank, privilege and esteem. An absent master wrote: "I wish to be remembered to all the servants, distinguishing Andrew as the head man and Katy as the mother of the tribe. Not forgetting Charlotte as the head of the culinary department nor Marcus as the Tubal Cain of the community, hoping that they will continue to set a good example and that the young ones will walk in their footsteps." The foreman, the miller and the smith were men of position and pride. The butler, the maid and the children's nurse were in continuous contact with the white household, enjoying the best opportunity to acquire its manners along with its discarded clothing. The field hands were at the foot of the scale, with a minimum of white contact and privileged only to plod, so to say, as brethren to the ox.

At all times in the South as a whole perhaps half of the slaves were owned or hired in units of twenty or less, which were too small for the full plantation order, and perhaps half of this half were on mere farms or in town employment, rather as "help" than as a distinct laboring force. Many small planters' sons and virtually all the farmers in person worked alongside any field hands they might possess; and indoor tasks were parceled among the women and girls white and black. As to severity of treatment, the travelers were likely to disagree. Schoepf and Stirling thought the farmers' slaves were in the better case, while Russell surmised the contrary. A Georgia physician found himself impelled to plead against over-incitement by small proprietors: "Men who own but few slaves and who share the labors of the field or workshop with them are very liable to deceive themselves by a specious process of reasoning. They say, 'I carry row for row with my negroes, and I put no more upon them than I take upon myself.' But the master who thus reasons is forgetful or ignorant of the great truth that the Negro's powers of endurance are really inferior to his; while in the case of the latter there is wanting those incentives to action that animate and actually *strengthen* the master."

However the case may have been as to relative severity on farms and plantations, there can be no doubt that the farmers' slaves of all sorts were likely to share somewhat intimately such lives as their masters led and to appropriate a considerable part of such culture as they possessed—to be more or less genteel with their gentility or crude with their crudity, to think similar thoughts and speak much the same language. On the other hand, the one instance of wide divergence in dialect between the whites and the Negroes prevailed in the single district in which the scheme of life was that of large plantations from the time when Africans were copiously imported. On the seaboard of South Carolina and Georgia most of the blacks (and they are very black) still speak Gullah, a dialect so distinct that unfamiliar visitors may barely understand it. And dialect, there as elsewhere, is an index to culture in general.

The life of slaves, whether in large groups or small, was not without grievous episodes. A planter's son wrote to his father upon a discovery of mislaid equipment: "The bridle and martingal which you whipped Amy so much for stealing was by some inattention of Robert's left in Mr. Clark's stable." Again, an overseer, exasperated by the sluggishness of his cook, set her to field work as discipline, only to have her demonstrate by dying that her protestations of illness had been true.

Grievances reinforced ennui to promote slacking, absence without leave, desertion and mutiny. The advertising columns of the newspapers bristled with notices of runaways; and no detailed plantation record which has come to my hand is without mention of them. As an extreme example, here is a summer's account by an overseer, or so much of it as can be deciphered: "August the 20 1844 Randle caught at Mr. Cathram brung home . . . [he had] left on the 12th July 1844 Lem runway on the 25 of July caught on the 2 of August by 1 of Mr Kings negroes Oscar runway on the 27 of August . . . George at tempt to git away I coat him and put a ringe and chane on him under the neck Lem runway on the 21 of August September the 3 Beny Bill Elijah Ellie all gowne together and Carline runway on the 3 stayed out 2 days . . . Joe runway on the 11th September."

Certain slaves were persistent absconders, and the chronic discontent of others created special problems for their masters. Thus a citizen in the Shenandoah Valley declined to hire one of his slaves to the proprietors of an iron furnace because "the previous bad character of the fellow in connection with recent declarations of his has left no doubt on my mind but he would make an effort to reach the State of Ohio, and by being placed at your Works it would certainly facilitate his object. Was I to send him I am persuaded that he would render you no services, and it might be the means of losing the fellow entirely." On the other hand, a mistress in the same locality sought an employer for her woman slave because "Ann has become very impudent and should be hired to a strict master who can handle her." But a strict master carried no guarantee of success, as an Alabama news item will show. William Pearce had notified an erring slave that a flogging was to be given him after supper. In due time Pearce called the man, who came from the kitchen with a pretense of submission, "but so soon as he got in striking distance drew an axe which had been concealed, and split in twain the head of his master."

part three
slavery and personality

six
sambo:
a non-
stereotype

STANLEY ELKINS

Stanley Elkins presents an original interdisciplinary assessment of slavery and its impact on the black personality in this selection. The controversy over his thesis is given in The Debate over Slavery: Stanley Elkins and His Critics *(1971), edited by Ann Lane. Critics have not accepted his major arguments for a subservient Sambo stereotype nor his concentration camp analogy; however, this provocative work merits close consideration. Elkins (b. 1925) received his doctorate from Columbia University (1959) and is professor of history at Smith College.*

It is hoped that the very hideousness of a special example of slavery has not disqualified it as a test for certain features of a far milder and more benevolent form of slavery.* But it should still be possible to say, with regard to the individuals who lived as slaves within the respective systems, that just as on one level there is every difference between a wretched childhood and a carefree one, there are, for other purposes, limited features which the one may be said to have shared with the other.

Both were closed systems from which all standards based on prior connections had been effectively detached. A working

Source: Stanley Elkins, *Slavery: A Problem in American Institutional and Intellectual Life* (Chicago: University of Chicago Press, 1959), pp. 128–39. Copyright © 1959 by The University of Chicago. Footnotes are omitted. Reprinted with permission.
* Elkins had described the effects on personality behavior of the environment of Nazi concentration camps, and compared personality types of both the concentration camp and the antebellum plantation.—Eds.

adjustment to either system required a childlike conformity, a limited choice of "significant others." Cruelty per se cannot be considered the primary key to this; of far greater importance was the simple "closedness" of the system, in which all lines of authority descended from the master and in which alternative social bases that might have supported alternative standards were systematically suppressed. The individual, consequently, for his very psychic security, had to picture his master in some way as the "good father," even when, as in the concentration camp, it made no sense at all. But why should it not have made sense for many a simple plantation Negro whose master did exhibit, in all the ways that could be expected, the features of the good father who was really "good"? If the concentration camp could produce in two or three years the results that it did, one wonders how much more pervasive must have been those attitudes, expectations, and values which had, certainly, their benevolent side and which were accepted and transmitted over generations.

For the Negro child, in particular, the plantation offered no really satisfactory father-image other than the master. The "real" father was virtually without authority over his child, since discipline, parental responsibility, and control of rewards and punishments all rested in other hands; the slave father could not even protect the mother of his children except by appealing directly to the master. Indeed, the mother's own role loomed far larger for the slave child than did that of the father. She controlled those few activities—household care, preparation of food, and rearing of children—that were left to the slave family. For that matter, the very etiquette of plantation life removed even the honorific attributes of fatherhood from the Negro male, who was addressed as "boy"—until, when the vigorous years of his prime were past, he was allowed to assume the title of "uncle."

From the master's viewpoint, slaves had been defined in law as property, and the master's power over his property must be absolute. But then this property was still human property. These slaves might never be quite as human as *he* was, but still there were certain standards that could be laid down for their behavior: obedience, fidelity, humility, docility, cheerfulness, and so on. Industry and diligence would of course be demanded, but a final element in the master's situation would undoubtedly qualify that expectation. Absolute power for him meant absolute dependency for the slave—the dependency not of the developing child but of the perpetual child. For the master, the role most aptly fitting such a relationship would naturally be that of the father. As a father he could be either harsh or kind, as he chose, but as a *wise* father he would have, we may suspect, a sense of the limits of his situation. He must be ready to cope with *all* the qualities of the child, exasperating as well as ingratiating. He might conceivably have to expect in this child—besides his loyalty, docility, humility, cheerfulness, and (under supervision) his diligence—such additional qualities as irresponsibility, playfulness, silliness, laziness, and (quite possibly) tendencies to lying and stealing. Should the entire prediction prove accurate, the result would be something resembling "Sambo."

The social and psychological sanctions of role-playing may in the last analysis prove to be the most satisfactory of the several approaches to Sambo, for, without doubt, of all the roles in American life that of Sambo was by far the most pervasive. The outlines of the role might be sketched in by crude necessity, but what of the finer shades? The sanctions against overstepping it were bleak enough, but the rewards—the sweet applause, as it were, for performing it with sincerity and feeling—were something to be appreciated on quite another level. The law, untuned to the deeper harmonies, could command the player to be present for the occasion, and the whip might even warn against his missing the grosser cues, but could those things really insure the performance that melted all hearts? Yet there was many and many a performance, and the audiences (whose standards were high) appear to have been for the most part well pleased. They were actually viewing their own masterpiece. Much labor had been lavished upon this chef d'oeuvre, the most genial resources of Southern society had been available for the work; touch after touch had been applied throughout the years, and the result—embodied not in the unfeeling law but in the richest layers of Southern lore—had been the product of an exquisitely rounded collective creativity. And indeed, in a sense that somehow transcended the merely ironic, it was a labor of love. "I love the simple and unadulterated slave, with his geniality, his mirth, his swagger, and his nonsense," wrote Edward Pollard. "I love to look upon his countenance shining with content and grease; I love to study his affectionate heart; I love to mark that peculiarity in him, which beneath all his buffoonery exhibits him as a creature of the tenderest sensibilities, mingling his joys and his sorrows with those of his master's home." Love, even on those terms, was surely no inconsequential reward.

But what were the terms? The Negro was to be a child forever. "The Negro . . . in his true nature, is always a boy, let him be ever so old. . . ." "He is . . . a dependent upon the white race; dependent for guidance and direction even to the procurement of his most indispensable necessaries. Apart from this protection he has the helplessness of a child—without foresight, without faculty of contrivance, without thrift of any kind." Not only was he a child; he was a happy child. Few Southern writers failed to describe with obvious fondness the bubbling gaiety of a plantation holiday or the perpetual good humor that seemed to mark the Negro character, the good humor of an everlasting childhood.

The role, of course, must have been rather harder for the earliest generations of slaves to learn. "Accommodation," according to John Dollard, "involves the renunciation of protest or aggression against undesirable conditions of life and the organization of the character so that protest does not appear, but acceptance does. It may come to pass in the end that the unwelcome force is idealized, that one identifies with it and takes it into the personality; it sometimes even happens that what is at first resented and feared is finally loved."

Might the process, on the other hand, be reversed? It is hard to imagine its being reversed overnight. The same role might still be played in the years after slavery—we are told that it was—and yet it was played to more vulgar audiences with cruder standards, who paid much less for what they saw. The lines might be repeated more and more mechanically, with less and less conviction; the incentives to perfection could become hazy and blurred, and the excellent old piece could degenerate over time into low farce. There could come a point, conceivably, with the old zest gone, that it was no longer worth the candle. The day might come at last when it dawned on a man's full waking consciousness that he had really grown up, that he was, after all, only playing a part.

One might say a great deal more than has been said here about mass behavior and mass manifestations of personality, and the picture would still amount to little more than a grotesque cartoon of humanity were not some recognition given to the ineffable difference made in any social system by men and women possessing what is recognized, anywhere and at any time, simply as character. With that, one arrives at something too qualitatively fine to come very much within the crude categories of the present discussion; but although it is impossible to generalize with any proper justice about the incidence of "character" in its moral, irreducible, individual sense, it may still be possible to conclude with a note or two on the social conditions, the breadth or narrowness of their compass, within which character can find expression.

Why should it be, turning . . . to Latin America, that there one finds no Sambo, no social tradition, that is, in which slaves were defined by virtually complete consensus as children incapable of being trusted with the full privileges of freedom and adulthood? There, the system surely had its brutalities. The slaves arriving there from Africa had also undergone the capture, the sale, the Middle Passage. They too had been uprooted from a prior culture, from a life very different from the one in which they now found themselves. There, however, the system was not closed.

Here again the concentration camp, paradoxically enough, can be instructive. There were in the camps a very small minority of the survivors who had undergone an experience different in crucial ways from that of the others, an experience which protected them from the full impact of the closed system. These people, mainly by virtue of wretched little jobs in the camp administration which offered them a minute measure of privilege, were able to carry on "underground" activities. In a practical sense the actual operations of such "undergrounds" as were possible may seem to us unheroic and limited: stealing blankets; "organizing" a few bandages, a little medicine, from the camp hospital; black market arrangements with a guard for a bit of extra food and protection for oneself and one's comrades; the circulation of news; and other such apparently trifling activities. But for the psychological balance of those involved, such activities were vital; they made possible a fundamentally different adjustment to the camp. To a prisoner so engaged, there were others who mattered, who gave real point to his existence—the SS was no longer the *only* one. Conversely, the role of the child was not the only one he played. He could take initiative; he could give as well as receive protection; he did things which had meaning in adult terms. He had, in short, alternative roles; this was a fact which made such a prisoner's transition from his old life to that of the camp less agonizing and destructive; those very prisoners, moreover, appear to have been the ones who could, upon liberation, resume normal lives most easily. It is, in fact, these people—not those of the ranks—who have described the camps to us.

It was just such a difference—indeed, a much greater one—that separated the typical slave in Latin America from the typical slave in the United States. Though he too had experienced the Middle Passage, he was entering a society where alternatives were significantly more diverse than those awaiting his kinsman in North America. Concerned in some sense with his status were distinct and at certain points competing institutions. This involved multiple and often competing "significant others." His master was, of course, clearly the chief one—but not the only one. There could, in fact, be a considerable number: the friar who boarded his ship to examine his conscience, the confessor; the priest who made the rounds and who might report irregularities in treatment to the *procurador*; the zealous Jesuit quick to resent a master's intrusion upon such sacred matters as marriage and worship (a resentment of no small consequence to the master); the local magistrate, with his eye on the king's official protector of slaves, who would find himself in trouble were the laws too widely evaded; the king's informer who received one-third of the fines. For the slave the result was a certain latitude; the lines did not all converge on one man; the slave's personality, accordingly, did not have to focus on a single role. He was, true enough, primarily a slave. Yet he might in fact perform multiple roles. He could be a husband and a father (for the American slave these roles had virtually no meaning); open to him also were such activities as artisan, peddler, petty merchant, truck gardener (the law reserved to him the necessary time and a share of the proceeds, but such arrangements were against the law for Sambo); he could be a communicant in the church, a member of a religious fraternity (roles guaranteed by the most powerful institution in Latin America—comparable privileges in the American South depended on a master's pleasure). These roles were all legitimized and protected *outside* the plantation; they offered a diversity of channels for the development of personality. Not only did the individual have multiple roles open to him as a slave, but the very nature of these roles made possible a certain range of aspirations should he some day become free. He could have a fantasy-life not limited to catfish and watermelons; it was within his conception to become a priest, an independent farmer, a successful merchant, a military officer. The slave could actually—to an extent quite unthinkable in the United States—conceive of himself *as a rebel*. Bloody slave revolts, actual wars, took place in Latin America; nothing on this order occurred in the United States. But even without a rebellion, society here had a network of customary arrangements, rooted in antiquity, which made possible at many points a smooth transition of status from slave to free and which provided much social space for the exfoliation of individual character.

To the typical slave on the ante-bellum plantation in the United States, society of course offered no such alternatives. But that is hardly to say that something of an "underground"—something rather more, indeed, than an underground—could not exist in Southern slave society. And there were those in it who hardly fitted the picture of "Sambo."

The American slave system, compared with that of Latin America, was closed and circumscribed, but, like all social systems, its arrangements were less perfect in practice than they appeared to be in theory. It was possible for significant numbers of slaves, in varying degrees, to escape the full impact of the system and its coercions upon personality. The house servant, the urban mechanic, the slave who arranged his own employment and paid his master a stipulated sum each week, were all figuratively members of the "underground." Even among those working on large plantations, the skilled craftsman or the responsible slave foreman had a measure of independence not shared by his simpler brethren. Even the single slave family owned by a small farmer had a status much closer to that of house servants than to that of a plantation labor gang. For all such people there was a margin of space denied to the majority; the system's authority-structure claimed their bodies but not quite their souls.

Out of such groups an individual as complex and as highly developed as William Johnson, the Natchez barber, might emerge. Johnson's diary reveals a personality that one recognizes instantly as a type—but a type whose values came from a sector of society very different from that which formed Sambo. Johnson is the young man on the make, the ambitious free-enterpriser of American legend. He began life as a slave, was manumitted at the age of eleven, and rose from a poor apprentice barber to become one of the wealthiest and most influential Negroes in ante-bellum Mississippi. He was respected by white and black alike, and counted among his friends some of the leading public men of the state.

It is of great interest to note that although the danger of slave revolts (like Communist conspiracies in our own day) was much overrated by touchy Southerners, the revolts that actually did occur were in no instance planned by plantation laborers but rather by Negroes whose qualities of leadership were developed well outside the full coercions of the plantation authority-system. Gabriel, who led the revolt of 1800, was a blacksmith who lived a few miles outside Richmond; Denmark Vesey, leading spirit of the 1822 plot at Charleston, was a freed Negro artisan who had been born in Africa and served several years aboard a slave-trading vessel; and Nat Turner, the Virginia slave who fomented the massacre of 1831, was a literate preacher of recognized intelligence. Of the plots that have been convincingly substantiated (whether they came to anything or not), the majority originated in urban centers.

For a time during Reconstruction, a Negro elite of sorts did emerge in the South. Many of its members were Northern Negroes, but the Southern ex-slaves who also comprised it seem in general to have emerged from the categories just indicated. Vernon Wharton, writing of Mississippi, says:

A large portion of the minor Negro leaders were preachers, lawyers, or teachers from the free states or from Canada. Their education and their independent attitude gained for them immediate favor and leadership. Of the natives who became their rivals, the majority had been urban slaves, blacksmiths, carpenters, clerks, or waiters in hotels and boarding houses; a few of them had been favored body-servants of affluent whites.

The William Johnsons and Denmark Veseys have been accorded, though belatedly, their due honor. They are, indeed, all too easily identified, thanks to the system that enabled them as individuals to be so conspicuous and so exceptional and, as members of a group, so few.

seven
rebels
and
sambos

KENNETH M. STAMPP

*Kenneth M. Stampp (b. 1912) is Morrison Professor of History at the
University of California, Berkeley. He earned his graduate degrees at
the University of Wisconsin (Ph.D., 1942). Among his many highly
regarded publications on the Civil War are* Indiana Politics in the
Civil War *(1949),* And the War Came *(1950), and the now classic
revisionist interpretation of slavery,* The Peculiar Institution *(1956).
Stampp's concept of the slave self-image and personality should be
compared with Elkins's portrait of Sambo.*

Since the Elkins thesis is familiar, I will only summarize the
three chief points of his strategy, which are (1) his use of
comparative history, (2) his use of personality theory, and (3)
his use of analogy. Elkins argues, first of all, that the Negro with
a Sambo-type personality was not a universal product of slavery
in the Americas but, because of certain unique conditions, a
peculiar product of slavery in the United States. The principal
differences between North American and Latin American slavery,
he believes, were the latter's relatively greater flexibility and
openness, the far greater opportunities it gave the Negro to
escape into free society, and the presence of not one but several
centers of authority: church and state as well as slave master. In
the antebellum South slavery grew unchecked by church or state;

Source: Kenneth M. Stampp, "Rebels and Sambos: The Search for the Negro
Personality," *Journal of Southern History* 37 (August 1971): 371–76, 378–88.
Footnotes omitted. Copyright © 1971 by the Southern Historical Association.
Reprinted by permission of the Managing Editor.

its form was dictated by the needs of the planter capitalists; and state laws treated the slave essentially as property, thus depriving him of his identity as a human being. Southern slavery operated as a "closed system" in which the slaves had only limited contacts with free society and little hope of becoming part of it. It was this closed system that produced Sambo.

Second, to explain how southern slavery had this devastating effect on the Negro, Elkins utilizes some of the literature on personality theory. Using Freud, he points to the impossibility of a "meaningful relationship between fathers and sons" and to the difficulty of becoming a man without "acceptable male models to pattern yourself after." But he relies chiefly on a blend of certain aspects of the interpersonal theory of Harry Stack Sullivan and of role psychology. Sullivan maintains that personality can be studied only as it manifests itself in interpersonal relations, and he stresses the manner in which personality is formed in relationships with so-called significant others—that is, with those in positions of authority or otherwise capable of enhancing or endangering one's security. Out of anxiety concerning the attitudes of these significant others a person learns to behave in ways that meet their expectations. Eventually, some of this behavior is internalized and becomes part of the personality. Role psychology emphasizes the roles, or models of behavior, that are extended to individuals throughout their lives by organizations, or by groups, or by society at large. There are rewards for playing the expected role well and penalties for playing it badly or not at all. How well an individual plays a role depends in part on his skill, on his motivation, on his "role knowledge," and on "role clarity," the last requiring a condition of general agreement about proper behavior. The more clearly a role is defined the better it is likely to be performed, and the greater its impact is likely to be on the personality of the performer. Thus, it may be that to some degree one's personality consists of the roles one plays.

Applying these ideas to the southern plantation slave, the Elkins hypothesis runs something like this: in a closed system from which there was virtually no escape, the master, whose authority was absolute, who dispensed rewards and punishments, was the only significant other in the slave's life. The master defined the slave's role, provided him with a clear and simple script, judged his performance, and rewarded him according to its quality. The result was Sambo, the perpetually dependent, irresponsible child. Elkins does not claim that Sambo was the universal slave personality, for he recognizes that there were "a great profusion of individual types." A "significant number," including house servants, skilled craftsmen, slaves who hired their own time, slave foremen, and those who lived in single families on small farms managed "to escape the full impact of the system and its coercions upon personality." For these slaves "there was a margin of space denied to the majority . . . ," and few of them took on the character of Sambo. But of the mass of field hands on large and small plantations, though Elkins recognizes that some did not fit the classic Sambo type, it is clearly his intention to suggest that Sambo embraced the majority.

Finally, to illuminate certain aspects of southern slavery, Elkins resorts to the analogy of the Nazi concentration camp. He warns that an analogy must not be taken literally, for things that are analogous are not identical. His purpose is to examine two situations which, in spite of their "vast dissimilarities," contain "mechanisms that are metaphorically comparable and analytically interchangeable." In this analogy the mechanism was "the infantilizing tendencies of absolute power." Elkins sees a rough similarity between the Sambo produced by slavery on the southern plantation and the human product of the concentration camp, whose experiences often led to personality disintegration, infantilization, and even a tendency to look on SS guards in a childlike way as father figures.

Both the master of the plantation and the commander of the concentration camp were the sole significant others in the lives of the people under their control. Both could mete out punishment or grant protection, while the slaves and inmates were reduced to complete dependence. "A working adjustment to either system," Elkins concludes, "required a childlike conformity . . ."; the crucial factor

. . . *was the simple "closedness" of the system, in which all lines of authority descended from the master. . . . The individual, consequently, for his very psychic security, had to picture his master in some way as the "good father," even when, as in the concentration camp, it made no sense at all. But why should it not have made sense for many a simple plantation Negro whose master did exhibit, in all the ways that could be expected, the features of the good father who was really "good"? If the concentration camp could produce in two or three years the result that it did, one wonders how much more pervasive must have been those attitudes, expectations, and values which had, certainly, their benevolent side and which were accepted and transmitted over generations.*

It is no small tribute to Elkins's achievement that his essay should have provided the focus for virtually all scholarly discussion of slave personality for the past decade and that a volume of commentary, with a response from Elkins, has recently been published. I doubt that any future historian of slavery will fail to recognize Sambo as an authentic personality type among the slaves on southern plantations. More generally, Elkins has contributed much to arousing interest in the problem of slave personality and to making historians aware of the possibility of dealing with the problem through an interdisciplinary approach. On the other hand, I believe that the discussion has been rather too much preoccupied with his hypothesis; that, in consequence, we have made little additional progress during the past decade; and that the time has come for renewed investigation. Elkins, after all, intended his essay to be the start of a new approach, suggestive rather than definitive; and, accordingly, he left plenty of work for others to do. Moreover, his essay contains a number of flaws, which give the remaining work a special urgency.

Because of their fascination with the essay's methodology and conceptualization, many scholars seem to have overlooked its lack of empirical evidence—its bland assumption that the prevalence of Sambo on the plantations can be taken for granted. The concentration-camp analogy, of course, proves nothing; at most, Elkins can argue that *if* the typical plantation slave was a Sambo, the literature on the camps might suggest an explanation of *why* he was a Sambo. Elkins, as I have noted, takes Sambo for granted because Sambo appears so prominently in antebellum plantation literature. But most of this literature was written by white men, and much of it is in defense of slavery. To accept it at face value would be only slightly more justifiable than to accept at face value a body of literature on the concentration camps written not by former inmates and competent scholars, such as Bruno Bettelheim, but by the SS guards. Moreover, the public testimony of white witnesses does not by any means invariably support the Elkins hypothesis, for contemporary writers often speak of the resourcefulness and guile of Negroes, and numerous essays on the governing of slaves warn masters never to trust them. Elkins is certainly mistaken when he asserts that the prevalence of Sambo was part of the Negro's own lore. Neither the slave narratives nor the Negro's oral tradition give validity to Sambo as the typical plantation slave; rather, their emphasis is on the slave dissemblers and the ways in which they deceived their masters.

In an essay on sources, Elkins explains why he did not use manuscript plantation records, which constitute the private testimony of the white slaveholders. Manuscripts, he writes, "are useful principally on questions of health and maintenance, and they have already been worked over with great care and thoroughness by eminent scholars." But the plantation manuscripts are in fact quite valuable for the study of slave personality, and even information on maintenance and health (including mental health) is decidedly relevant. If the manuscripts have been worked over by other scholars, that is really of little help to Elkins, because no one has used them for precisely his purpose and with his hypothesis in mind. He offers no explanation for his failure to examine other sources, especially newspapers, with their extremely revealing fugitive-slave advertisements, and contemporary periodicals, with their countless essays on the management of slaves and their descriptions of slave behavior. As a result, Elkins is obliged in the end to offer corroborating testimony from sources such as John Pendleton Kennedy's *Swallow Barn* (1832), where we learn that the slave had "the helplessness of a child—without foresight, without faculty of contrivance, without thrift of any kind"; and from Edward Pollard's *Black Diamonds Gathered in the Darkey Homes of the South* (1859), which assures us that "The Negro . . . in his true nature, is always a boy, let him be ever so old. . . ." "Few Southern writers," Elkins concludes, "failed to describe with obvious fondness . . . the perpetual good humor that seemed to mark the Negro character, the good humor of an everlasting childhood."

David C. McClelland, one of Elkins's authorities on personality, devotes two chapters of his book to the problems of collecting and interpreting data. In one of them, McClelland observes that an individual's personality may change "as he changes or as the scientist's insights improve." This is an important point, for the accumulation of an ample supply of data is often the beginning of improved insight. Eugene D. Genovese, after paying tribute to Elkins's achievement, reminds us "that all psychological models may only be used suggestively for flashes of insight or as aids in forming hypotheses and that they cannot substitute for empirical investigation." . . .

Turning finally to the theoretical foundation of the Elkins essay, the important question is whether personality theory, when applied to the available data, points unmistakably to Sambo as the typical plantation slave. This does not seem to be the case, for there are important aspects of the theories that Elkins uses, together with much data, that suggest other plausible hypotheses. In addition, personality theory contains more than a few ambiguities. For example, role psychology does not provide a clear answer to the question of whether the Sambo role played by many plantation slaves was internalized and became part of their personalities, or whether it was a form of conscious hypocrisy, a mere accommodation to the system. David McClelland asserts that the roles an individual plays are part of his knowledge "and therefore part of his personality." But Ralph Linton thinks that playing a role proves nothing about an individual's personality, "except that he has normal learning ability." The psychologist must be able "to penetrate behind the façade of social conformity and cultural uniformity to reach the authentic individual." Two recent writers on role theory, Theodore R. Sarbin and Vernon L. Allen, illustrating a new trend, hardly touched on the matter of role and personality. They are far more interested in the interaction between role and social identity, and they state explicitly that they "are not using 'social identity' and 'self' as synonyms. Selfhood . . . embodies more residuals of behavior than those generated through role enactment."

At times Elkins approaches this problem warily, suggesting only that the roles an individual plays are internalized to "an extent," or that "deliberate" role-playing and "natural" role-playing grade into each other "with considerable subtlety." Returning to the problem in an appendix, Elkins again refuses to generalize: "The main thing I would settle for would be the existence of a broad belt of indeterminacy between 'mere acting' and the 'true self' "; to the extent that they "grade into one another" it seems "permissible to speak of Sambo as a personality 'type.' "

These cautious statements are hardly disputable, but they do not represent the tone of the essay as a whole. The clear inference to be drawn from Elkins's comparison of North American and Latin American slavery, from his introduction of the concentration-camp analogy, and from his use of personality theory is that Sambo was not a dissembler but a distinct personality type and the typical plantation slave. Indeed, in one footnote, Elkins explicitly rejects the possibility that the Sambo role was only a form of conscious accommodation. Not until after emancipation, he insists, did the Negro's "moral and psychological orientation" permit the development of "the essentially intermediate technique of accommodation . . . as a protective device beneath which a more independent personality might develop."

Yet the theory of role psychology, when applied to the information we have concerning the life and behavior of plantation slaves, provides plenty of room for personalities other than Sambo. This theory, which stresses the importance of "role clarity," holds that adequate role performance will be unlikely if there is uncertainty concerning the nature of an appropriate role. In addition, role conflict occurs when a person finds himself occupying more than one status at a given time, each requiring different behavior, or when there is more than one source of advice about how a role is properly played. Conflicting obligations or conflicting expectations may lead to a personal crisis and to difficulty in playing any role successfully. These were problems that troubled plantation slaves in their daily lives—problems whose psychic strains they resolved in ways that varied with their individual natures and experiences.

Harry Stack Sullivan's model of interpersonal relationships, when fully utilized, also provides theoretical support for a variety of plantation slave personalities. Sullivan describes a highly complex and subtle interplay between an individual and the significant others in his life. One side of it—the side that Elkins explores—is the anxiety that helps to mold an individual's personality as he behaves in certain ways to meet the expectations of authority figures. But there is another side, which involves the conscious manipulation of significant others to the individual's own advantage. By the time a child is ready for school, Sullivan observes, he has "evolved techniques" for handling his parents "with only a modicum of pain"; he now encounters other adults "who have to be managed." In addition to manipulation, there is still another and less fortunate way that a person deals with tendencies in his personality that are strongly disapproved by his significant others. These tendencies are neither lost nor resolved but simply "dissociated from personal awareness." In the process of dissociation they are "excluded from the self" and become part of the "extra-self." But the tendencies still remain an integral part of the personality, manifesting "themselves in actions, activities, of which the person himself remains quite unaware."

Sullivan's concept of dissociation describes a condition which, at a certain point, may lead to serious psychic problems. Generally speaking, he believes that the "healthy development of personality is inversely proportionate to the amount, to the number, of tendencies which have come to exist in dissociation." In Elkins's conceptualization we encounter the significant other of Sullivan's interpersonal theory but not the phenomena of manipulation and dissociation; yet all three concepts are relevant to the problem of slave personality.

I believe that a historian utilizing the available evidence on slave behavior and master-slave relationships and taking account of all aspects of the personality theories used by Elkins will be forced to abandon his hypothesis that Sambo was the typical plantation slave. Several historians have already briefly suggested other possibilities, and at present several have more ambitious projects under way. The following is my own sketch of an alternative to the Elkins hypothesis.

I would begin by accepting Elkins's description of southern slavery as a closed system from which few escaped and in which the slaves had only limited contacts with free society; his emphasis on the dehumanizing tendencies of slavery (though not in North America alone); his belief that the system had built into it powerful pressures toward dependent, infantilized, emasculated personalities; and his conception of the master as a formidable significant other in the life of nearly every slave—partly an object of fear, partly a Freudian father figure. But I would reject his assertions that the master's power was absolute; that he was the only significant other in the lives of his slaves; that he was the sole author of the role, or roles, they played; and that southern slaves were almost totally dehumanized. Finally, I would suggest that plantation slaves encountered significant others in their own families and communities; that dissembling, manipulation, dissociation, role conflict, and lack of role clarity were important ingredients of slave behavior; and that plantation life enabled most slaves to develop independent personalities—indeed, provided room for the development of a considerable range of personality types.

In his concentration-camp analogy Elkins observes that a small minority of the inmates, who held minor administrative jobs, was able to escape the full impact of the system on personality. This minority could engage in petty underground activities, such as stealing blankets, getting medicine from the camp hospital, and negotiating black-market arrangements with the guards. These activities turned out to be crucial for the fortunate prisoner's psychological balance. For him the SS was not the only significant other, and the role of the child was not the only one open to him—he was able to do things that had meaning in adult terms.

If these trivial activities could preserve the psychic balance of camp inmates, then the plantations afforded the great mass of field hands infinitely greater opportunities to preserve theirs. Though plantation slaves were exposed to influences that encouraged childlike dependency and produced emasculated personalities, the system nevertheless permitted them a degree of semiautonomous community life and the opportunity to do many things that had meaning in adult terms. They lived in their own separate quarters where they could escape the constant scrutiny of their masters. Unlike the slaves on the sugar and coffee plantations of Brazil and Cuba, where men outnumbered women by as much as three to one, those on the plantations of the Old South could experience something like a normal sex life, because the sexes were usually evenly divided. Though slave marriages had no legal support and families were ever in danger of being broken up by sales, southern slaves nevertheless lived in family groups more often than those on the commercialized plantations of Latin America. In fact, it was customary for them to live in family groups.

Slave families, because of their relative lack of economic significance, their instability, and the father's severely restricted role, may well have been less important in the lives of slaves than the broader plantation slave communities. The latter provided opportunities for self-expression in their celebrations of holidays, in their music and folklore, and in other aspects of community life. Historians have perhaps viewed religion among plantation slaves too much in terms of the nonreligious uses to which it was put. We know that masters used religious indoctrination as a means of control and that slaves found in their religious services subtle ways of protesting their condition. But there were other and deeper ways in which religion served them. It provided a system of beliefs that comforted and sustained them in their bondage, and it afforded additional means of self-expression that helped them retain their psychic balance. I do not believe that a truly autonomous Afro-American subculture developed in slavery days, but some of the ingredients for one were certainly there.

Both the family and the community provided plantation slaves with roles other than that defined by the master, and with significant others besides the master. For the very young child the mother, not the master, was the significant other in the sense that Sullivan uses this concept. Though the near impossibility of fathers acting as true authority figures was of great psychic importance, meaningful relationships did sometimes exist between fathers and sons. As the child grew, the master's role as a significant other became increasingly vital, but he was always in competition with significant others in the slave community: with husbands, wives, fathers, and mothers; with religious leaders; with strong male models, some of whom may even on occasion have served as substitute father figures; with slaves believed to possess mystical powers; and with those whose wisdom was respected. Few planters had any illusions about being the only authority figures on their estates; as one of them noted, there were always slaves who held "a kind of magical sway over the minds and opinions of the rest."

In his community, in the presence of these significant others, the slave could play a role decidedly different from the one prescribed by his master. This situation often led to the psychologically important problem of role conflict. An obvious illustration is the dilemma of a slave being questioned by his master concerning the whereabouts of a fugitive. Here the rules of proper conduct that the master tried to instill in him came in conflict with the values of his community. If we can trust the testimony of the masters themselves, community values usually triumphed, even though punishment might be the consequence.

Was there any sense in which the master's power was really absolute? Only in the sense that if a master killed a slave by overwork, or by cruel punishment, or in a fit of rage, it was nearly impossible to convict him in a court of law. But southern state laws did not themselves give the master absolute power over his slaves, for the laws recognized their humanity and attempted to control the degree of punishment that might be inflicted, the amount of labor that could be required, and the care that was to be provided. Where the laws failed, the master might be restrained by his own moral standards or by those of the white community. If law and custom were not enough, he was still confronted by the fact that, unlike the inmates of a concentration camp, his slaves had monetary value and a clear purpose—to toil in his fields—and therefore had bargaining power. The master got work out of his slaves by coercion, by threats, by promises of rewards, by flattery, and by a dozen other devices he knew of. But if he were prudent, he knew that it was not wise to push slaves too far—to work them too long, punish them too severely or too often, or make too many threats. Slaves had their own standards of fair play and their own ways of enforcing them. The relationship between master and slave was not one in which absolute power rested on one side and total helplessness on the other; rather, the relationship was one of everlasting tensions, punctuated by occasional conflicts between combatants using different weapons.

If the master had the *de facto* power of life and death over his slaves, the slaves knew that he was most unlikely to use it. They knew that rules, infractions and certain forms of resistance did not ordinarily lead to death but to milder and often quite bearable forms of punishment, or to sale to another master, or, on occasion, to no penalty at all. In the conflicts between masters and slaves, the masters or their overseers sometimes suffered defeat, and the resulting collapse of discipline led inflexibly to economic disaster. To read the essays "On the Management of Negroes" that frequently appeared in southern periodicals is to appreciate the practical limits of the master's power. Clearly, for the slave, as he responded to the problems of his existence, the choices open to him were a good deal more complex than a simple one between life and death.

Role psychology, as those who have written on the subject observe, tempts one to view the whole problem metaphorically as drama. But in slavery the theatrical situation was seldom one in which the master wrote the script and the slaves played their roles and read their lines precisely as their master had written them. The instructions masters gave to their overseers, which describe the qualities they hoped to develop in their slaves, suggest something quite different. Significantly, the model slave described in these instructions is not Sambo but a personality far more complicated. Masters wanted their slaves, like Sambo, to be docile, humble, and dependent; but they also wanted them to be diligent, responsible, and resourceful—in short, as Earle E. Thorpe has noted, "to give a very efficient and adult-like performance." The slaves in turn had to find ways to resolve the obviously incongruent role expectations of their masters, and many of them responded as persons troubled with this or other forms of role conflict often do. They resorted to lying and deceit.

Eugene Genovese, in an otherwise valuable essay on slave personality, is not very perceptive when he argues that slaves who tricked their masters, rather than coping with problems of role conflict and role definition, were merely playing a game which the masters enjoyed and had themselves written into the script. True, a master might occasionally be amused when a house servant outwitted him, but there is scant evidence that he enjoyed this "game" when played by field hands. This was certainly not in the script, and masters frequently expressed their anger or perplexity at the "untrustworthiness" of Negroes. Their appreciation of the slave trickster was confined mostly to their public defenses of slavery and to sentimental plantation literature. In private they were seldom amused.

Plantation field hands, finding no escape from slavery but plenty of elbow room within it, usually managed to preserve their individuality and therefore revealed a considerable variety of personality types. Among the types, there were, to be sure, genuine Sambos who seemed to have internalized much of the role, for some slaves simply lacked the psychic strength to withstand the infantilizing pressures of the system. They looked on the master as a father figure, accepted his values, identified with him, and perhaps even viewed themselves through his eyes.

We may assume that the slave who internalized the Sambo role did accept his master as his only significant other and that he was relatively untroubled by the problem of role conflict. But he must have been sorely disturbed by the psychic process of dissociation—that is, exclusion from the self of disapproved personality tendencies, which then become part of what Sullivan calls the "extra-self." Such dissociated tendencies, we must remember, still remain part of the personality; and, therefore, Sambo was Sambo only up to a point—in Genovese's words, "up to the moment that the psychological balance was jarred from within or without. . . ." Plantation records often reveal the astonishment of masters when slaves, who had long given evidence of Sambo personalities, suddenly behaved in disturbingly un-Sambo ways.

Another personality type was evident on certain large plantations, especially on those of absentee owners in new areas of the Southwest, where labor was sometimes exploited ruthlessly and punishments were brutal. This type displayed none of the silliness of Sambo, none of his childlike attachment to master or overseer; rather, he was profoundly apathetic, full of depression and gloom, and seemingly less hostile than indifferent toward the white man who controlled him. One slaveholder observed that slaves subjected to overwork and cruel punishments were likely to fall "into a state of impassivity" and to become "insensible and indifferent to punishment, or even to life. . . ." These brutalized slaves had their counterparts on Latin American plantations, where extreme cruelty produced in some a state of psychic shock manifested in apathy and depression. In colonial Brazil this condition was sufficiently common to be given a special name: *banzo.* It is this condition that seems to be analogous to the concentration camps, where life had lost its meaning, and to prisons and asylums, where "situational withdrawal" is a form of institutional adaptation.

More numerous among plantation personalities were the men and women with sufficient strength of character to escape the emasculating tendencies of the system, a group whose size Elkins seriously underestimates. These slaves were not only not Sambos, but they did not *act* like Sambos—their behavior was in no respect infantile. Though observing all the niceties of interracial etiquette, they maintained considerable dignity even in their relations with their masters. Judging from plantation diaries, masters often treated slaves of this kind with genuine respect and seldom made the mistake of regarding them as children. Slaves such as these were not troublemakers; they were rarely intransigent as long as what was asked of them and provided for them was reasonable by their standards. They worked well and efficiently and showed considerable initiative and self-reliance. They tended to be fatalistic about their lot, expected little of life, and found their satisfaction in the religious and social activities of the slave communities. No doubt their psychic balance and their relative tranquillity was sometimes disturbed by a certain amount of role conflict; and they could hardly have escaped the phenomenon of dissociation described by Sullivan.

Rebels must also be included among those whose personalities were far removed from the traditional Sambo. I would not limit these to the organizers of or participants in rebellions, for their number was very small. Rather, I would include all who were never reconciled to the system and engaged in various acts of resistance: running away, arson, the damaging of crops and tools, and sometimes even assaults on masters, overseers, or other whites. Needless to say, it is often impossible to distinguish conscious resistance from the unconscious carelessness and indifference of slaves, but the evidence of genuine resistance is clear enough in some cases. Genovese argues that the slaves did not develop a genuine revolutionary tradition, that their acts of resistance were usually nihilistic, and that at best they came out of slavery with a tradition of recalcitrance—"of undirected, misdirected or naively directed violence." George M. Fredrickson and Christopher Lasch object even to calling the acts of slave rebels "resistance" and insist that it was only "intransigence." They define the former as organized, purposeful political action, the latter as mere "personal strategy of survival" which can easily lead to "futile and even self-destructive acts of defiance." Surely, little that was done by the rebels could form the basis for a revolutionary tradition or satisfy so narrow a definition of resistance; but these were rebels, nonetheless, who never internalized the masters' standards of good conduct and never dissociated from their conscious selves all the disapproved tendencies of their personalities.

All of these slaves types, with myriad individual variations, were recognizable on the plantations. But I believe that the personalities of most slaves are less easily classified, because their behavior when observed by whites was usually that of conscious accommodators. They played the role of Sambo with varying degrees of skill and consistency, but, in contrast to the authentic Sambos, most characteristics of the role did not become part of their true personalities. For them the Sambo routine was a form of "ritual acting"—that is, they went through the motions of the role, but with a rather low degree of personal involvement.

eight
the black ethos
in slavery

STERLING STUCKEY

*Sterling Stuckey (b. 1932), who received a Ph.D. from Northwestern
University and is currently associate professor of history at
Northwestern, is the author of* The Ideological Origins of Black
Nationalism. *He has long emphasized the need to integrate black
studies into our educational systems. Through his exploration of slave
songs and black folklore Stuckey has provided a portion of the empirical
data so necessary to an investigation of the slave psyche. Stuckey's
research leads him to conclude that the dehumanized slave of Elkins's
work was not typical of plantation slavery. However, the reader must
consider whether this inquiry into slave consciousness is the conclusion or
merely the beginning of the slave personality controversy.*

My thesis, which rests on an examination of folk songs and tales,
is that slaves were able to fashion a life style and set of
values—an ethos—which prevented them from being imprisoned
altogether by the definitions which the larger society sought to
impose. This ethos was an amalgam of Africanisms and New
World elements which helped slaves, in Guy Johnson's words,
"feel their way along the course of American slavery, enabling
them to endure. . . ." As Sterling Brown, that wise student of
Afro-American culture, has remarked, the values expressed in
folklore acted as a "wellspring to which slaves" trapped in the
wasteland of American slavery "could return in times of doubt to
be refreshed." In short, I shall contend that the process of
dehumanization was not nearly as pervasive as Stanley Elkins

Source: Sterling Stuckey, "Through the Prism of Folklore: The Black Ethos in
Slavery," reprinted from *The Massachusetts Review* (Summer, 1968): 418–32.
Copyright © 1968, The Massachusetts Review, Inc. Reprinted by permission of
the publisher.

would have us believe; that a very large number of slaves, guided by this ethos, were able to maintain their essential humanity. I make this contention because folklore, in its natural setting, is of, by and for those who create and respond to it, depending for its survival upon the accuracy with which it speaks to needs and reflects sentiments. I therefore consider it safe to assume that the attitudes of a very large number of slaves are represented by the themes of folklore.

Frederick Douglass, commenting on slave songs, remarked his utter astonishment, on coming to the North, "to find persons who could speak of the singing among slaves as evidence of their contentment and happiness." The young DuBois, among the first knowledgeable critics of the spirituals, found white Americans as late as 1903 still telling Afro-Americans that "life was joyous to the black slave, careless and happy." "I can easily believe this of some," he wrote, "of many. But not all the past South, though it rose from the dead, can gainsay the heart-touching witness of these songs."

They are the music of an unhappy people, of the children of disappointment; they tell of death and suffering and unvoiced longing toward a truer world, of misty wanderings and hidden ways.

Though few historians have been interested in such wanderings and ways, Frederick Douglass, probably referring to the spirituals, said the songs of slaves represented the sorrows of the slave's heart, serving to relieve the slave "only as an aching heart is relieved by its tears." "I have often sung," he continued, "to drown my sorrow, but seldom to express my happiness. Crying for joy, and singing for joy, were alike uncommon to me while in the jaws of slavery."

Sterling Brown, who has much to tell us about the poetry and meaning of these songs, has observed: "As the best expression of the slave's deepest thoughts and yearnings, they (the spirituals) speak with convincing finality against the legend of contented slavery." Rejecting the formulation that the spirituals are mainly otherworldly, Brown states that though the creators of the spirituals looked toward heaven and "found their triumphs there, they did not blink their eyes to trouble here." The spirituals, in his view, "never tell of joy in the 'good old days'. . . . The only joy in the spirituals is in dreams of escape."

Rather than being essentially otherworldly, these songs, in Brown's opinion, "tell of this life, of 'rollin' through an unfriendly world!" To substantiate this view, he points to numerous lines from spirituals: "Oh, bye and bye, bye and bye, I'm going to lay down this heavy load"; "My way is cloudy"; "Oh, stand the storm, it won't be long, we'll anchor by and by"; "Lord help me from sinking down"; and "Don't know what my mother wants to stay here fuh, Dis ole world ain't been no friend to huh." To those scholars who "would have us believe that when the Negro sang of freedom, he meant only what the whites meant, namely freedom from sin," Brown rejoins:

Free individualistic whites on the make in a prospering civilization, nursing the American dream, could well have felt their only bondage to be that of sin, and freedom to be religious salvation. But with the drudgery, the hardships, the auction

block, the slave-mart, the shackles, and the lash so literally present in the Negro's
experience, it is hard to imagine why for the Negro they would remain figurative. The
scholars certainly did not make this clear, but rather take refuge in such dicta as: "the
slave never contemplated his low condition."

"Are we to believe," asks Brown, "that the slave singing 'I been rebuked, I been
scorned, done had a hard time sho's you bawn,' referred to his being outside the true
religion?" A reading of additional spirituals indicates that they contained distinctions in
meaning which placed them outside the confines of the "true religion." Sometimes, in
these songs, we hear slaves relating to divinities on terms more West African than
American. The easy intimacy and argumentation, which come out of a West African
frame of reference, can be heard in "Hold the Wind."

When I get to heaven, gwine be at ease,
Me and my God gonna do as we please.

gonna chatter with the Father, argue with the Son,
Tell um 'bout the world I just come from. (*Emphasis added.*)

If there is a tie with heaven in those lines from "Hold the Wind," there is also a
clear indication of dislike for the restrictions imposed by slavery. And at least one high
heavenly authority might have a few questions to answer. *Tell um 'bout the world I just*
come from makes it abundantly clear that some slaves—even when released from the
burdens of the world—would keep alive painful memories of their oppression.

If slaves could argue with the son of God, then surely, when on their knees in prayer,
they would not hesitate to speak to God of the treatment being received at the hands of
their oppressors.

Talk about me much as you please, (2)
Chillun, talk about me much as you please,
Gonna talk about you when I get on my knees.

That slaves could spend time complaining about treatment received from other slaves
is conceivable, but that this was their only complaint, or even the principal one, is
hardly conceivable. To be sure, there is a certain ambiguity in the use of the word
"chillun" in this context. The reference appears to apply to slaveholders.

The spiritual, *Samson*, as Vincent Harding has pointed out, probably contained much
more (for some slaves) than mere biblical implications. Some who sang these lines from
Samson, Harding suggests, might well have meant tearing down the edifice of slavery. If
so, it was the ante-bellum equivalent of today's "burn baby burn."

He said, 'An' if I had-'n my way,'
He said, 'An' if I had-'n my way,'
He said, 'An' if I had-'n my way,'
I'd tear the build-in' down!'

He said, 'And now I got my way, (3)
And I'll tear this buildin' down.'

    Both Harriet Tubman and Frederick Douglass have reported that some of the spirituals carried double meanings. Whether most of the slaves who sang those spirituals could decode them is another matter. Harold Courlander has made a persuasive case against widespread understanding of any given "loaded" song, but it seems to me that he fails to recognize sufficiently a further aspect of the subject: slaves, as their folktales make eminently clear, used irony repeatedly, especially with animal stories. Their symbolic world was rich. Indeed, the various masks which many put on were not unrelated to this symbolic process. It seems logical to infer that it would occur to more than a few to seize upon some songs, even though created originally for religious purposes, assign another meaning to certain words, and use these songs for a variety of purposes and situations.

    At times slave bards created great poetry as well as great music. One genius among the slaves couched his (and their) desire for freedom in a magnificent line of verse. After God's powerful voice had "Rung through Heaven and down in Hell," he sang, "My dungeon shook and my chains, they fell."

    In some spirituals, Alan Lomax has written, Afro-Americans turned sharp irony and "healing laughter" toward heaven, again like their West African ancestors, relating on terms of intimacy with God. In one, the slaves have God engaged in a dialogue with Adam:

'Stole my apples, I believe.'
'No, marse Lord, I spec it was Eve.'
Of this tale there is no mo'
Eve et the apple and Adam de co'.

    Douglass informs us that slaves also sang ironic seculars about the institution of slavery. He reports having heard them sing: "We raise de wheat, dey gib us de corn; We sift de meal, dey gib us de huss; We peal de meat, dey gib us de skin; An dat's de way dey take us in." Slaves would often stand back and see the tragicomic aspects of their situation, sometimes admiring the swiftness of blacks:

Run, nigger, run, de patrollers will ketch you,
Run, nigger run, it's almost day.
Dat nigger run, dat nigger flew;
Dat nigger tore his shirt in two.

And there is:

My ole mistiss promise me
W'en she died, she'd set me free,
She lived so long dat 'er head got bal'
An' she give out'n de notion a-dyin' at all.

In the ante-bellum days, work songs were of crucial import to slaves. As they cleared and cultivated land, piled levees along rivers, piled loads on steamboats, screwed cotton bales into the holds of ships, and cut roads and railroads through forest, mountain and flat, slaves sang while the white man, armed and standing in the shade, shouted his orders. Through the sense of timing and coordination which characterized work songs well sung, especially by the leaders, slaves sometimes quite literally created works of art. These songs not only militated against injuries but enabled the bondsmen to get difficult jobs done more easily by not having to concentrate on the dead level of their work. "In a very real sense the chants of Negro labor," writes Alan Lomax, "may be considered the most profoundly American of all our folk songs, for they were created by our people as they tore at American rock and earth and reshaped it with their bare hands, while rivers of sweat ran down and darkened the dust."

Long summer day makes a white man lazy,
    Long summer day.
Long summer day makes a nigger run away, sir,
    Long summer day.

Other slaves sang lines indicating their distaste for slave labor:

Ol' massa an' ol' missis,
Sittin' in the parlour,
Jus' fig'in' an' a-plannin'
How to work a nigger harder.

And there are these bitter lines, the meaning of which is clear:

Missus in the big house,
Mammy in the yard,
Missus holdin' her white hands,
Mammy workin' hard (3)
Missus holdin' her white hands,
Mammy workin' hard.

Old Marse ridin' all time,
Niggers workin' round,
Marse sleepin' day time,
Niggers diggin' in the ground, (3)
Marse sleepin' day time,
Niggers diggin' in the ground.

Courlander tells us that the substance of the work songs "ranges from the humorous to the sad, from the gentle to the biting, and from the tolerant to the unforgiving." The statement in a given song can be metaphoric, tangent or direct, the meaning personal or impersonal. "As throughout Negro singing generally, there is an incidence of social criticism, ridicule, gossip, and protest." Pride in their strength rang with the downward thrust of axe—

When I was young and in my prime, (hah!)
Sunk my axe deep every time, (hah!)

Blacks later found their greatest symbol of manhood in John Henry, descendant of Trickster John of slave folk tales:

A man ain't nothing but a man,
But before I'll let that steam driver beat me down
I'll die with my hammer in my hand.

   Though Frances Kemble, an appreciative and sensitive listener to work songs, felt that "one or two barbaric chants would make the fortune of an opera," she was on one occasion "displeased not a little" by a self-deprecating song, one which "embodied the opinion that 'twenty-six black girls not make mulatto yellow girl,' and as I told them I did not like it, they have since omitted it." What is pivotal here is not the presence of self-laceration in folklore, but its extent and meaning. While folklore contained some self-hatred, on balance it gives no indication whatever that blacks, as a group, liked or were indifferent to slavery, which is the issue.
   To be sure, only the most fugitive of songs sung by slaves contained direct attacks upon the system. Two of these were associated with slave rebellions. The first, possibly written by ex-slave Denmark Vesey himself, was sung by slaves on at least one island off the coast of Charleston, S.C., and at meetings convened by Vesey in Charleston. Though obviously not a folksong, it was sung by the folk.

Hail! all hail! ye Afric clan,
Hail! ye oppressed, ye Afric band,
Who toil and sweat in slavery bound
And when your health and strength are gone
Are left to hunger and to mourn,
Let independence be your aim,
Ever mindful what 'tis worth.
Pledge your bodies for the prize,
Pile them even to the skies!

The second, a popular song derived from a concrete reality, bears the marks of a conscious authority:

You mought be rich as cream
And drive you coach and four-horse team,
But you can't keep de world from moverin' round
Nor Nat Turner from gainin' ground.

And your name it mought be Caesar sure,
And got you cannon can shoot a mile or more,
But you can't keep de world from moverin' round
Nor Nat Turner from gainin' ground.

The introduction of Denmark Vesey, class leader in the A.M.E. Church, and Nat Turner, slave preacher, serves to remind us that some slaves and ex-slaves were violent as well as humble, impatient as well as patient.

It is also well to recall that the religious David Walker, who had lived close to slavery in North Carolina, and Henry Highland Garnett, ex-slave and Presbyterian minister, produced two of the most inflammatory, vitriolic and doom-bespeaking polemics America has yet seen. There was theological tension here, loudly proclaimed, a tension which emanated from and was perpetuated by American slavery and race prejudice. This dimension of ambiguity must be kept in mind, if for no other reason than to place in bolder relief the possibility that a great many slaves and free Afro-Americans could have interpreted Christianity in a way quite different from white Christians.

Even those songs which seemed most otherworldly, those which expressed profound weariness of spirit and even faith in death, through their unmistakable sadness, were accusatory, and God was not their object. If one accepts as a given that some of these appear to be almost wholly escapist, the indictment is no less real. Thomas Wentworth Higginson came across one—". . . a flower of poetry in that dark soil," he called it.

I'll walk in de graveyard, I'll walk through de graveyard,
To lay dis body down.
I'll lie in de grave and stretch out my arms,
Lay dis body down.

Reflecting on "I'll lie in de grave and stretch out my arms," Higginson said that "Never, it seems to me, since man first lived and suffered, was his infinite longing for peace uttered more plaintively than in that line."

There seems to be small doubt that Christianity contributed in large measure to a spirit of patience which militated against open rebellion among the bondsmen. Yet to overemphasize this point leads one to obscure a no less important reality: Christianity, after being reinterpreted and recast by slave bards, also contributed to that spirit of endurance which powered generations of bondsmen, bringing them to that decisive moment when for the first time a real choice was available to scores of thousands of them.

When that moment came, some slaves who were in a position to decide for themselves did so. W. E. B. DuBois re-created their mood and the atmosphere in which they lived:

There came the slow looming of emancipation.
Crowds and armies of the unknown, inscrutable,
unfathomable Yankees; cruelty behind and before;

rumors of a new slave trade, but slowly,
continuously, the wild truth, the bitter truth,
the magic truth, came surging through. There
was to be a new freedom! And a black nation
went tramping after the armies no matter what
it suffered; no matter how it was treated, no
matter how it died.

The gifted bards, by creating songs with an unmistakable freedom ring, songs which would have been met with swift, brutal repression in the ante-bellum days, probably voiced the sentiments of all but the most degraded and dehumanized. Perhaps not even the incredulous slavemaster could deny the intent of the new lyrics. "In the wake of the Union Army and in the contraband camps," remarked Sterling Brown, "spirituals of freedom sprang up suddenly. . . . Some celebrated the days of Jubilo: 'O Freedom; O Freedom!' and 'Before I'll be a slave, I'll be buried in my grave!, and 'Go home to my lord and be free.' " And there was: " 'No more driver's lash for me. . . . Many thousand go.' "

DuBois brought together the insights of the poet and historian to get inside the slaves:

There was joy in the South. It rose like perfume—like a prayer. Men stood quivering.
Slim dark girls, wild and beautiful with wrinkled hair, wept silently; young women,
black, tawny, white and golden, lifted shivering hands, and old and broken mothers,
black and gray, raised great voices and shouted to God across the fields, and up to the
rocks and the mountains.

Some sang:

Slavery chain done broke at last, broke at last, broke at last,
Slavery chain done broke at last,
Going to praise God till I die.

I did tell him how I suffer,
In de dungeon and de chain,
And de days I went with head bowed down,
And my broken flesh and pain,
Slavery chain done broke at last, broke at last, broke at last.

Whatever the nature of the shocks generated by the war, among those vibrations felt were some that had come from Afro-American singing ever since the first Africans were forcibly brought to these shores. DuBois was correct when he said that the new freedom song had not come from Africa, but that "the dark throb and beat of that Ancient of Days was in and through it." Thus, the psyches of those who gave rise to and provided widespread support for folk songs had not been reduced to *tabula rasa* on which a slave-holding society could at pleasure sketch out its wish fulfillment fantasies.

We have already seen the acute degree to which some slaves realized they were being exploited. Their sense of the injustice of slavery made it so much easier for them to act out their aggression against whites (by engaging in various forms of "day to day" resistance) without being overcome by a sense of guilt, or a feeling of being ill-mannered. To call this nihilistic thrashing about would be as erroneous as to refer to their use of folklore as esthetic thrashing about. For if they did not regard themselves as the equals of whites in many ways, their folklore indicates that the generality of slaves must have at least felt superior to whites morally. And that, in the context of oppression, could make the difference between a viable human spirit and one crippled by the belief that the interests of the master are those of the slave.

part four
slave
resistance

nine
day to day
resistance
to slavery

RAYMOND A. BAUER and ALICE H. BAUER

*Raymond A. Bauer and Alice H. Bauer did their research on slave
resistance under the direction of the well-known anthropologist Melville
J. Herskovits. The Bauers' article, published in the* Journal of Negro
History *(1942), led the way in demonstrating that slave resistance did
not always take the form of armed revolts. Therefore, they argue, the
rather infrequent number of revolts could not be taken as evidence of
slave docility.*

The Negroes were well aware that the work they did benefited
only the master. "The slaves work and the planter gets the
benefit of it." "The conversation among the slaves was that they
worked hard and got no benefit, that the masters got it all." It is
thus not surprising that one finds many recurring comments that
a slave did not do half a good day's work in a day. A northerner
whom Lyell met in the South said:

> *Half the population of the south is employed in seeing that the other
> half do their work, and they who do work, accomplish half what they
> might do under a better system.*

An English visitor, with a very strong pro-slavery bias
corroborates this:

Source: Raymond A. Bauer and Alice H. Bauer, "Day to Day Resistance to
Slavery," *Journal of Negro History* 27 (October 1942): 391–93, 397–404, 406–7,
417–19. Copyright © by The Association for the Study of Negro Life and
History, Inc. Reprinted by permission of the author and the publisher.

> *The amount of work expected of the field hand will not be more than one half of what would be demanded of a white man; and even that will not be properly done unless he be constantly overlooked. . . .*

Just how much of this was due to indifference and how much due to deliberate slowing up is hard to determine. Both factors most probably entered. A worker who had to devote himself to a dull task from which he can hope to gain nothing by exercising initiative soon slips into such a frame of mind that he does nothing more than go through the motions. His chief concern is to escape from the realities of his task and put it in the back of his mind as much as possible.

There is, indeed, a strong possibility that this behavior was a form of indirect aggression. While such an hypothesis cannot be demonstrated on the basis of the available contemporary data, it is supported by Dollard's interpretation of similar behavior which he found in southern towns:

> *If the reader has ever seen Stepin Fetchit in the movies, he can picture this type of character. Fetchit always plays the part of a well-accommodated lower-class Negro, whining, vacillating, shambling, stupid, and moved by very simple cravings. There is probably an element of resistance to white society in the shambling, sullenly slow pace of the Negro; it is the gesture of a man who is forced to work for ends not his own and who expresses his reluctance to perform under these circumstances. . . .*

The amount of slowing up of labor by the slaves must, in the aggregate, have caused a tremendous financial loss to plantation owners. The only way we have of estimating it quantitatively is through comparison of the work done in different plantations and under different systems of labor. The statement is frequently made that production on a plantation varied more than 100 percent from time to time. Comparison in the output of slaves in different parts of the South also showed variations of over 100 percent. Most significant is the improvement in output obtained under the task, whereby the slaves were given a specific task to fulfill for their day's work, any time left over being their own. . . .

The indifference of the slaves to the welfare of the masters extended itself to a complete contempt for property values. The slaves were so careless with tools that they were equipped with special tools, and more clumsy than ordinary ones:

> *The nigger hoe was first introduced into Virginia as a substitute for the plow, in breaking up the soil. The law fixes its weight at four pounds,—as heavy as the woodman's axe. It is still used, not only in Virginia, but in Georgia and the Carolinas. The planters tell us, as the reason for its use, that the negroes would break a Yankee hoe in pieces on the first root, or stone that might be in their way. An instructive commentary on the difference between free and slave labor!*
>
> *The absence of motive, and the consequent want of mental energy to give vigor to the arm of the slave is the source of another great drawback upon the usefulness of his labour. His implements or tools are at least one-third (in some instances more than twofold) heavier and stronger than the northern man's to counteract his want of skill*

*and interest in his work. A Negro hoe or scythe would be a curiosity to a New
England farmer.*

Not only tools but live stock suffered from the mistreatment by the slaves. Olmsted
found not only the "nigger hoe" but even discovered that mules were substituted for
horses because horses could not stand up under the treatment of the slaves:

> *I am shown tools that no man in his senses, with us, would allow a laborer, to
> whom he was paying wages, to be encumbered with; and the excessive weight and
> clumsiness of which, I would judge, would make work at least ten percent greater than
> those ordinarily used with us. And I am assured that, in the careless and clumsy way
> they must be used by the slaves, anything lighter or less crude could not be furnished
> them with good economy, and that such tools as we constantly give our laborers and
> find profit in giving them, would not last out a day in a Virginia corn-field—much
> lighter and more free from stones though it be than ours.*
>
> *So, too, when I ask why mules are so universally substituted for horses on the farm,
> the first reason given, and confessedly the most conclusive one, is, that horses cannot
> bear the treatment they always must get from negroes; horses are always soon
> foundered or crippled by them but mules will bear cudgeling, and lose a meal or two
> now and then, and not be materially injured, and they do not take cold or get sick if
> neglected or overworked. But I do not need to go further than to the window of the
> room in which I am writing, to see, at almost any time, treatment of cattle that would
> insure the immediate discharge of the driver, by almost any farmer owning them in
> the North.*

Redpath verifies Olmsted's statement—by telling how he saw slaves treat stock. It is
important to note that Redpath was a strong abolitionist and most sympathetic toward
the slaves:

> *He rode the near horse, and held a heavy cowhide in his hand, with which from
> time to time he lashed the leaders, as barbarous drivers lash oxen when at work.
> Whenever we came to a hill, especially if it was very steep, he dismounted, lashed the
> horses with all his strength, varying his performances by picking up stones, none of
> them smaller than half a brick, and throwing them with all his force, at the horses'
> legs. He seldom missed.*
>
> *The wagon was laden with two tons of plaster in sacks.*
>
> *This is a fair specimen of the style in which Negroes treat stock.*

The indifference to livestock is well illustrated by an incident which Olmsted
recounts:

> *I came, one afternoon, upon a herd of uncommonly fine cattle as they were being
> turned out of a field by a negro woman. She had given herself the trouble to let down
> but two of the seven bars of the fence, and they were obliged to leap over a barrier at
> least four feet high. Last of all came, very unwillingly, a handsome heifer, heavy with*

*calf; the woman urged her with a cudgel and she jumped, but lodging on her belly, as
I came up she lay bent, and, as it seemed, helplessly hung upon the top bar. . . . The
woman struck her severely and with a painful effort she boggled over.*

In the Sea Islands off the coast of Georgia, Kemble reported that the slaves started
immense fires, destroying large sections of woods through carelessness or maliciousness.

*The "field hands" make fires to cook their midday food wherever they happen to be
working, and sometimes through their careless neglect, but sometimes, too, undoubtedly
on purpose, the woods are set fire to by these means. One benefit they consider . . . is
the destruction of the dreaded rattlesnakes.*

The slaves on Lewis's West Indies plantation let cattle get into one of his best
cane-pieces because they neglected to guard them, being more interested in a dance
which was going on. They were fully aware that the cattle were ruining the sugar cane,
but kept right on singing and dancing. Lewis was able to get only a handful of house
servants to drive the cattle out of the cane, and that not until the cane-piece was ruined.

One tobacco planter complained that his slaves would cut the young plants
indiscriminately unless they were watched. When it became late in the season and there
was need of haste to avoid frost they would work only the thickest leaving the sparser
ones untouched. Another planter said that he could cultivate only the poorer grades of
tobacco because the slaves would not give necessary attention to the finer sort of
plants. . . .

But not only did the Negro slaves refuse to work, and not only did they destroy
property, but they even made it impossible for planters to introduce new work
techniques by feigning clumsiness. They prevented the introduction of the plow in this
way on many plantations. Olmsted here cites many instances. Lewis, quoted in
Plantation Documents found the same thing to be true in Jamaica.

*It appears to me that nothing could afford so much relief to the negroes, under the
existing system of Jamaica, as the substituting of labor of animals for that of slaves in
agriculture wherever such a measure is practicable. On leaving the island, I impressed
this wish of mine upon the mind of my agents with all my power; but the only result
has been the creating a very considerable expense in the purchase of ploughs, oxen and
farming implements; the awkwardness and still more the obstinacy of the few negroes,
whose services were indispensable, was not to be overcome; they broke plough after
plough, and ruined beast after beast, till the attempt was abandoned in despair.*

Malingering was a well-known phenomenon throughout the slave states. The
purpose of feigning illness was generally to avoid work, although occasionally a slave
who was being sold would feign a disability either to avoid being sold to an undesirable
master, or to lower his purchase price so as to obtain revenge on a former master. The
women occasionally pretended to be pregnant, because pregnant women were given
lighter work assignments and were allowed extra rations of food.

In a situation such as this in which physical disability was an advantage, one would expect much malingering. One might also expect to find functional mental disorders, hysterical disorders which would get one out of work. There is some evidence that many had such functional disorders:

> *There are many complaints described in Dr. Cartwright's treatise, to which the Negroes, in slavery, seem to be peculiarly subject.*
>
> *Negro-consumption, a disease almost unknown to medical men of the Northern States and of Europe, is also sometimes fearfully prevalent among the slaves. "It is of importance," says the Doctor, "to know the pathognomic signs in its early stages, not only in regard to its treatment but to detect impositions, as negroes, afflicted with this complaint are often for sale; the acceleration of the pulse, on exercise, incapacitates them for labor, as they quickly give out, and have to leave their work. This induces their owners to sell them, although they may not know the cause of their inability to labor. Many of the negroes brought South, for sale, are in the incipient stages of this disease; they are found to be inefficient laborers, and sold in consequence thereof. The effect of superstition—a firm belief that he is poisoned or conjured—upon the patient's mind, already in a morbid state (dyaesthesia), and his health affected from hard usage, overtasking or exposure, want of wholesome food, good clothing, warm, comfortable lodging, with the distressing idea (sometimes) that he is an object of hatred or dislike, both to his master or fellow-servants, and has no one to befriend him, tends directly to generate that erythism of mind which is the essential cause of negro consumption" . . . "Remedies should be assisted by removing the original cause of the dissatisfaction or trouble of mind, and by using every means to make the patient comfortable, satisfied and happy."*

Of course it is impossible to determine the extent of these disorders. Assuming that Dr. Cartwright's assumption was correct, very few observers would be qualified to make an adequate diagnosis, and a very small proportion of these would be inclined to accept his interpretation. After all, functional disorders are in many cases almost impossible to tell from real disorders or from feigning, and since the behavior which Cartwright describes could very easily be interpreted on another, and easier, level by a less acute observer.

Of the extent to which illness was feigned there can, however, be little doubt. Some of the feigning was quite obvious, and one might wonder why such flagrant abuses were tolerated. The important thing to remember is that a slave was an important economic investment. Most slave owners sooner or later found out that it was more profitable to give the slave the benefit of the doubt. A sick slave driven to work might very well die. . . .

The patterns of resistance to slavery studied in this paper are: (1) deliberate slowing up of work; (2) destruction of property, and indifferent work; (3) feigning illness and pregnancy; (4) injuring one's self; (5) suicide; (6) a possibility that a significant number of slave mothers killed their children.

The motivation behind these acts was undoubtedly complex. The most obvious of the motives was a desire to avoid work. It has been demonstrated that the slaves were acutely conscious of the fact that they had nothing to gain by hard work except in those instances where they were working under the task system. The destruction of property and the poor quality of the slaves' work was mainly due to their indifference to their tasks. There is enough evidence that they could, and did, work hard and well when sufficiently motivated to refute any contention that the Negro slaves were congenitally poor workers.

Many of the slaves reacted to the institution of slavery in a far more drastic fashion than could be manifested by a mere desire to avoid work. Some of these slaves committed suicide; others killed members of their families, usually their children, in order that they might not grow up as slaves.

Possibly the most significant aspect of these patterns of resistance is the aggression against the white masters they imply. Unfortunately, however, though this aspect may be the most significant, it is the least subject to proof. On the plane of logic, there is every reason to believe that a people held in bondage would devise techniques such as have been described above as an indirect means of retaliation. . . .

The material presented here suggests the need for a reconsideration of the concept of the Negro's easy adjustment to slavery. He was not a cheerful, efficient worker, as has been assumed. Rather, he was frequently rebellious, and almost always sullen, as any person faced with a disagreeable situation from which he cannot escape will normally be. Nor can the belief that racial inferiority is responsible for inefficient workmanship on his part be supported. For such deficiencies of his workmanship as he manifested, or, indeed, may still be manifested, are seen to be explainable in terms that are in no sense to be couched in the conventional mold of inherent racial differences.

ten
plantation christianity: catalyst or opiate?

VINCENT HARDING

Vincent Harding (b. 1931) received his Ph.D. from the University of Chicago in 1965. Among his writings are "You've Taken My Nat and Gone," in William Styron's Nat Turner: Ten Black Writers Respond *(1968) and* Must Walls Divide *(1965). Dr. Harding demonstrates how the slaves interpreted Christianity as a revolutionary ideology justifying slave revolts despite the attempts of plantation owners to use the religion to inculcate docility and acceptance of bondage. Professor Harding is presently director of the Institute of the Black World in Atlanta.*

In his *Black Religion*, Joseph Washington wrote, "the religion of the Negro folk was chosen to bear roles of both protest and relief." Indeed Washington went on to suggest that "the uniqueness of black religion" since the days of slavery was to be found in its constant and often risky search for "the elusive but ultimate goal of freedom and equality by means of protest and action." Like so much of Washington's work, those last phrases may be overstatement, but they help to balance the scales set by Frazier, Mays and Marx.

Source: Vincent Harding, "Religion and Resistance among Antebellum Negroes, 1800–1860," in August Meier and Elliott M. Rudwick, eds., *The Making of Black America* vol. I (New York: Atheneum, 1969), pp. 181–90. Without footnotes. Reprinted with permission of the author.

Perhaps, then, this paper can be thought of as an attempt to suggest pathways towards an historical documentation of Joseph Washington's intuitive thesis, at least that part of it which seeks to appreciate the proper relationship of black religion to Negro protest and resistance. Without such an attempt we shall be in danger of fruitlessly trying to apply the religion of Ulrich Phillips's Negroes to the defiant men and women who often leap out of the pages of Aptheker and Stampp. To quote Douglass slightly out of context, "we can entertain no such nonsense as this . . ." (Even Marxists came to realize that religious commitment might produce revolutionary action. Those who claim to be unhindered by the fetters of ideology can do no less.)

It has seemed wise for the present to confine this statement to the period 1800–1860, and to focus on Negroes in the South. Therefore it may be significant to note that it was in 1800 that South Carolina's legislature indicated a keen awareness of the possible connections between black rebellion and black religion, an awareness that was apparently the property of many southern white persons. In that year the legislature passed one of the first of those countless 19th century laws restricting black religious services. This one forbade Negroes

> . . . *even in company with white persons to meet together and assemble for the purpose of . . . religious worship, either before the rising of the sun or after the going down of the same.*

Magistrates were given the power to break up all such gatherings. Behind the legislation was obviously a fear that these religious meetings might lead to trouble, especially if they were held at hours when they could not easily be monitored.

If the fear needed substantiation it was soon available. In Virginia's Henrico county Tom Prosser's slave, Gabriel, and Gabriel's brother, Martin, were then gathering slaves and free Negroes at strange hours and making strange uses of "religious services." Gabriel was plotting insurrection, and building a force that had evidently mounted into the thousands by 1800. At their religious services it was said that both Martin and Gabriel—what fitting names!—regularly set forth

> . . . *an impassioned exposition of Scripture . . . The Israelites were glowingly portrayed as a type of successful resistance to tyranny; and it was argued, that now, as then, God would stretch forth his arm to save, and would strengthen a hundred to overthrow a thousand.*

The black men of Henrico county were the new Israelites. Gabriel was their Moses. Would they follow?

It is not known how deeply this appeal from the Old Testament moved the persons who gathered in those secret meetings, nor which of them joined the attempted rebellion in response to it. But the analogy to the Israelites was a traditional one in the black community, and it continued to have great force among the slaves. Therefore it would not be too much to expect that some of the men who set themselves on the path of rebellion in those Virginia meetings were responding to a profoundly religious call, as well as to the news from Santo Domingo, or to the stirring cries of "Death or

Liberty." Haiti was a good example, and the political motto was a moving cry, but it surely helped to believe as well that the God of Israel would "stretch forth his arm" to intervene on behalf of the blacks.

When the insurrection was foiled by the sudden downpour of torrential rains, the white residents of Virginia would, of course, have been justified in thinking that divine intervention was indeed present—on their side. But they were likely caused to be suspicious about other religious matters as the trials of the rebels revealed that Methodists and Quakers—as well as Frenchmen—were to be spared the vengeful swords of Gabriel's band. What could that mean?

Religion and its relationship to black rebellion continued to be a matter for concern and for questions in Virginia, even before the coming of Nat Turner. For instance, one Richard Byrd of that state wrote to his Governor in May, 1810, to express his conviction that "slave preachers used their religious meetings as veils for revolutionary schemes," and he cited a "General Peter" from Isle of Wight as an example of the danger.

Six years later this kind of fear was given solid ground in the Old Dominion again, but it was a white preacher who now seemed to be using black religion for seditious purposes. George Boxley, proprietor of a county store, was a regular participant in the religious meetings held by the Negroes of Spottsylvania and Louisa counties. Soon he began telling them "that a little white bird had brought him a holy message to deliver his fellowmen from bondage . . ." Again the promise of divinely aided deliverance found active response, and Phillips says that Boxley "enlisted many blacks in his project" for messianic insurrection. Unfortunately for the black believers, as was so often the case, the plot was betrayed. Some Negro followers were hanged, others were sold out of the state, but Boxley escaped from jail. Perhaps the message of deliverance had been meant only for him. After all, it was a white bird.

The pattern of religious connections to rebellious movements continued consistently into South Carolina in the same year—1816. There, in Camden, a plot had evidently been maturing, and when the almost inevitable betrayal and arrests finally came, a local newspaper offered its own version of the relationship between religion and resistance:

It is a melancholy fact [*the editor said*] *that those who were most active in the conspiracy occupied a respectable stand in one of the churches, several were professors* [*i.e., avowed Christians*], *and one a class leader.*

Camden was not the only place in South Carolina where black Christians and class leaders were making life difficult for the keepers of the established order. Charleston was having its difficulties with the darker variety of Methodists, trouble that would eventually lead into deep distress.

The Negroes in the port city's Methodist congregations had long outnumbered their white brethren by ten to one. They had known a sense of significant independence through their own quarterly conference and as a result of the control they exercised over finances and the discipline of their members. In 1815 alleged "abuses" had led to the loss of these privileges as well as much of the independence that went with them. But black church leaders like Denmark Vesey, Peter Poyas and Jack Pritchard (Gullah Jack) had no intentions of accepting such debilitating penalties without offering direct and open response.

They led agitation among the Negro members, rounded up a thousand new members and sent two of their leaders up to Philadelphia to be ordained by the African Methodist Episcopal bishops there. Then in 1818 a dispute over their burial ground provided the occasion for more than 4000 of the 6000 black Methodists to withdraw their membership *en masse* from the white Charleston congregations. With ordained ministers of their own they now moved ahead to build a meeting house and establish an independent congregation called the African Church of Charleston.

It is in this context that we may speak more precisely of rebellion. Here the crucial issue is not the nature of what happened in 1822, not the matter of whether widely organized insurrection was being planned. At this juncture it is of critical importance simply to see that organized rebellion on another level had already been built deeply into the structure of black church life in Charleston. The agitation from 1815 to 1818 and the concerted withdrawal from the white congregations in the latter year took significant courage for the slaves. The raising of an independent house of worship implied not only the gathering of financial resources, but it was clearly an act of defiance for the world to see. The municipal officials knew this and responded accordingly with harassments, arrests, banishments, and finally with the closing of the church in 1821. It is, then, essential to note that the sense of black solidarity was imbedded in the organization of the Negro church. Attempts to dilute this or break it down met inevitably with resistance, resistance centered in that church's life.

Did the defiance include a wider plan for insurrection? It is not the purpose of this essay to enter into the argument that has been interestingly raised by Mr. Wade. However, my own examination of available evidence leads me to suspect that the plot was "more than loose talk by aggrieved and embittered men." These men had already given evidence of impressive skill in organizing black discontent for action. They had followers in their defiance, and their leadership was evidently trusted. There was no reason for them to be content with "loose talk" by 1822.

Whatever the extent of the new action being planned, it seems clear that some continuing organizing was going on, that it was centered in the membership of the African Church and that the charismatic Denmark Vesey was at the heart of the affair. Now, for our purposes it is necessary only to continue to deal with the role of religion as it participated in a movement that went beyond the defense of church-oriented prerogatives to new and likely bolder concerns. If, as seems probable, an insurrection was being planned, Vesey surely knew how to continue to use themes that had led the blacks to organize for independent church status.

His focus was regularly on religion. One witness testified that this leader's "general conversation . . . was about religion, which he would apply to slavery." Indeed, "all his religious remarks were mingled with slavery," according to the testimony. Was this surprising? For the most part these were church members who were being addressed, and they were also slaves. What other focus was more natural? These were also persons whose extant religious records indicate that they were profoundly attracted to the analogy between their condition and the condition of the Hebrews in Egypt. As a class leader, Vesey surely knew all this very well. So one of the alleged conspirators was probably quite accurate when he said that Denmark Vesey "read to us from the Bible, how the *children of Israel were delivered out of Egypt from bondage* . . ." Nor did the persuasive exhorter stop there. It is said that he made it clear to the bondsmen that it was imperative to their faith that slaves "attempt their emancipation, 'however shocking and bloody might be the consequences.' " And on the strength of his magnificent authority as a class leader—and as a man—he declared that such efforts would be "pleasing to the Almighty," and that their success was thereby guaranteed.

If, as we are suggesting, religion did play a critical role in the motivating of his followers, then Vesey chose wisely (or was fortunate, if he did not make the choice himself) when he gained an accomplice like Jack Pritchard, better known as Gullah Jack. This black man of Angolan background provided an excellent counterpoint to Vesey's Old Testament theme. For he was not only a member of the African Church but a conjurer, a medicine man in the African tradition. Therefore Vesey had the best of both religious worlds, and we are told that Gullah Jack exerted tremendous influence over the other members of his ancestral group.

This, of course, does not mean that Vesey did not seek to rally his forces through the use of other issues as well. The tradition of Santo Domingo, the debate over Missouri, the general mistreatment of the Negroes by the city authorities and by some of their masters—these were all part of the strategy. But it would be derelict to fail to note how crucial was the religious issue, especially in the light of the post-1814 church experiences. Was this not the significance of the note found in Peter Poyas's trunk after he was arrested: "Fear not, the Lord God that delivered Daniel is able to deliver us."

Then in the summer of 1822, when deliverance appeared to have been aborted and the gallows were heavy with black bodies, it was fitting that the city should demolish the First African Church. This was not only a rehearsal of more modern southern church treatment, but it was a testimony to the significant role the people of that congregation had played in carrying the contagion of rebellion. Nor was it surprising that an Episcopalian minister boasted that such things could never happen among black Episcopalians because their Negroes "were not allowed to exhort or expound scriptures in words of their own . . . and to utter . . . whatever nonsense might happen into their minds."

Regardless of how we see such matters now, it was evidently clear to most Charlestonians of the time that "religious enthusiasm" had been one of the motivating forces in Vesey's action. So all preachers of the gospel to slaves—white and black—were suspect. And a Charleston editor condemned the white Christian missionaries who

> . . . with the *Sacred Volume of God* in one hand scattered with the other the *firebrands of discord and destruction; and* secretly *dispensed among our Negro Population, the seeds of discontent and sedition.*

Though he saw much, the editor did not see that the firebrands and the seeds were often in the same hand as "the Sacred Volume," but he surely must have known that the hands were often black.

At least this was the case with Nat Turner, who carried his own Volume, fire and seeds. Whatever doubts we may entertain about the authenticity of Vesey's rebellion,

Turner leaves us with no choice. Even more important for our present concerns is the central theme of Turner's *Confession*—the theme of a black, avenging Messiah, urged into action by nothing less than the repeated calling of God. Here was religion and resistance that would not be separated.

Based primarily on the *Confession*, the story develops. As a child he became convinced that he was "intended for some great purpose." Evidently he nurtured the search for his destiny through arduous prayer and fasting and the development of an austere personal life. Turner claimed to be directed many times by "the Spirit" as it spoke to him in his lonely vigils or as he worked in the fields. A major theme of that direction was "Seek ye the kingdom of Heaven and all things shall be added unto you." When asked later about this "Spirit," the 31-year-old prisoner made it clear that he stood self-consciously in the prophetic tradition, for he said that he had been visited by "The Spirit that spoke to the Prophets in former days."

Eventually the young mystic became fully confirmed in his sense of ordination to some "great purpose in the hands of the Almighty," and he went through his own Wilderness experience—thirty days in the forests of Virginia as a runaway slave. Then the Spirit drove him back for his great encounter with the future. In 1825 Turner saw his first major vision suggestively describing his ultimate calling. White and black spirits were battling in the air. Thunder rang out, the sun was darkened, and he watched in awe as blood flowed through the land. The same Spirit promised him the wisdom and strength needed for the task.

After a fascinating variety of other visions, the critical revelation came in May, 1828. According to Nat,

I heard a loud noise in the heavens and the Spirit instantly appeared to me and said the Serpent was loosened, and Christ had laid down the Yoke he had borne for the sins of men, and that I should take it on and fight against the Serpent, for the time was fast approaching when the first should be last and the last should be first.

The Spirit also revealed to him that there would be adequate signs in nature to let him know when he should begin the messianic work for which he was ordained, when to "arise and prepare myself to slay my enemies with their own weapons." In an eclipse of the sun—that most ancient of signs—Nat Turner found his signal to begin. He ate a last supper with some of his followers and went forth to carry out his own version of the work of Christ, using the weapons of the Old Testament, drenching the ground with blood, for "neither age nor sex was to be spared." And when he was asked if he thought himself mistaken as he faced execution at the end, Turner's response came fittingly enough: "Was not Christ crucified?" To the charge of dastardly crime, his plea, of course, was "Not Guilty."

Obviously Nat Turner was one of those religious charismatics who arise in a variety of settings, from the walls of Münster to the fields of Southampton County. He was not a "preacher" in any formal sense of the word, and evidently belonged to no structured church group. But he was an "exhorter," and he clearly convinced his fellow slaves by the power of his message and the strange sense of his presence that he was the anointed one of God for their deliverance—a deliverance for which slaves never ceased to yearn.

No other explanation will open the intricacies of Nat Turner. Thus when they were wounded and waiting to die, it was said of his companions that some of them "in the aggonies [sic] of Death declared that they was going happy fore that God had a hand in what they had been doing . . ." They still believed that "Prophet Nat" was sent from God.

When all the dyings were over, after the fierce retaliations had taken place, the conviction and the legend lived on. Black people believed and remembered, and some acted. The religion of Nat Turner, the religion of black rebellion became part of their tradition. Whites, on the other hand, believed variations of the black themes and acted in their own ways. Their response was well summed up by a writer in the Richmond *Enquirer* who said then:

The case of Nat Turner warns us. No black man ought to be permitted to turn a preacher through the country. The law must be enforced—or the tragedy of Southampton appeals to us in vain.

In the minds of blacks and whites alike religion and rebellion had been welded into one terrifying—or exalting—reality through the black body of Nat Turner.

So the laws set off by fear swept through the states, forbidding Negroes to preach, in many places interdicting all meetings, attempting as it were to exorcise so troubling a religious spirit. The Mississippi law of 1831 provided a good example when it ruled that "It is 'unlawful for any slave, free Negro, or mulatto to preach the gospel' under pain of receiving thirty-nine lashes upon the naked back of the . . . preacher."

The laws did not stop the strange gospel of freedom from infiltrating into the ranks of the slaves—partly because it was already there. So an insurrectionary attempt came to light in Duplin County, North Carolina, in the fall of 1831, even before Turner had been captured. In the course of its account a newspaper article revealed that "a very intelligent negro preacher named David, was put on his trial . . . and clearly convicted . . ." as one of the ringleaders. Elsewhere in that same year another newspaper correspondent says, "It is much to be regretted that [the apparent wave of insurrectionary attempts] are instigated by fierce, ignorant fanatics, assuming to be preachers." His comment closed with this prophecy: "I forsee that this land must one day or other, become a field of blood." Thus in the mind of at least one man, black preachers of religion might well lead a people to bloody revolution. Strange opium.

In 1833 when Frederick Douglass, still a slave, tried to organize a Sabbath School class among the black young people of the Eastern Shore of Maryland, he found out that these white co-religionists had not yet disassociated themselves from earlier memories and convictions. Two Methodist class leaders led the mob that stormed Douglass's Sabbath School and Douglass said he was told by one Methodist that "I wanted to be another Nat Turner, and that, if I did not look out, I should get as many balls in me as Nat did into him."

Two years later, during the slave insurrection scare in Mississippi, it was again said that "suspicion centered around the 'itinerant preachers' " and other troublemakers in the neighborhood. In New Orleans the newspapers were complaining in 1839 about a Negro church which was "the greatest of all public nuisances and den for hatching plots against [the] masters." Seven years later the same problem existed in the city as the police arrested twelve Negroes in "a makeshift church" and charged them with "the habit of repairing to this place for . . . singing hymns and cantiques which was followed by sermons the subject of which was the most inflammatory character." Firebrands and sermons were continually being combined by black men whose religion had not yet made them "otherworldly" enough to suit the authorities.

It may be that the ambiguous nature of American religion, as it related to antebellum blacks, was best seen by a visitor to this land, one who had become a heroic figure among abolitionists by 1841. This was Joseph Cinquez, the African who had led a rebellion aboard the vessel, *Amistad*, as it carried a load of slaves along the coast of Cuba in 1839. In the course of the revolt the captain and the cook had been killed by the rebels, the ship was steered to American shores and Cinquez had been brought to New England with his fellow slaves. There they were exposed to American Christianity with all of its contradictory potentials.

Then, in 1841, just before leaving for his native continent Cinquez was given the rare opportunity to apply this nation's religion to his rebellion—after the fact. One of his fellow rebels said to a group of Christians, "We owe everything to God; he keeps us alive and makes us free." Filled with enthusiasm, another went on to claim that he would now pray for the captain and cook rather than kill them if the rebellion were to be done over again. We are told that "Cinquez, hearing this, smiled and shook his head. When asked if we would not pray for them, he said: 'Yes I would pray for 'em, an' kill 'em too.' "

part five
expansion, profits, and civil war

eleven
the natural
limits of
slavery expansion

CHARLES W. RAMSDELL

Charles W. Ramsdell (1877–1942) was president of the Mississippi Valley Historical Society (1928–1929) and president of the Southern Historical Association (1936). He was coeditor of the well-known History of the South *and on the editorial boards of the* Southwestern History Quarterly, *the* Mississippi Valley Historical Review, *and the* Journal of Southern History. *He taught at the University of Texas. Ramsdell was a part of the "needless war" school of Civil War history dominating the 1930s which blamed abolitionist agitation and political incompetence for the war. Here Ramsdell explores the agricultural, economic, and political conditions in the South which he believes would have caused the natural decline of slavery eventually, making the Civil War unnecessary.*

The causes of the expansion of slavery westward from the South Atlantic Coast are now well understood. The industrial revolution and the opening of world markets had continually increased the consumption and demand for raw cotton, while the abundance of fertile and cheap cotton lands in the Gulf States had steadily lured cotton farmers and planters westward. Where large-scale production was possible, the enormous demand for a steady supply of labor had made the use of slaves inevitable, for a sufficient supply of free labor was unprocurable on the frontier.

Source: Charles W. Ramsdell, "The Natural Limits of Slavery Expansion," *Mississippi Valley Historical Review* 16 (September 1929): 153–62, 166–71. Footnotes omitted. Copyright 1929 by the Organization of American Historians. Reprinted by permission of the publisher.

Within one generation, the cotton-growing slave belt had swept across the Gulf region from eastern Georgia to Texas. A parallel movement had carried slaves, though in smaller ratio to whites, into the tobacco and hemp fields of Kentucky, Tennessee, and Missouri. The most powerful factor in the westward movement of slavery was cotton, for the land available for other staples—sugar, hemp, tobacco—was limited, while slave labor was not usually profitable in growing grain. This expansion of the institution was in response to economic stimuli; it had been inspired by no political program nor by any ulterior political purpose. It requires but little acquaintance with the strongly individualistic and unregimented society of that day to see that it would have been extremely difficult, if not impossible, to carry out such an extensive program; nor is there any evidence that such a program existed. There was incentive enough in the desire of the individual slaveowner for the greater profits which he expected in the new lands. The movement would go on as far as suitable cotton lands were to be found or as long as there was a reasonable expectation of profit from slave labor, provided, of course, that no political barrier was encountered.

The astonishing rapidity of the advance of the southern frontier prior to 1840 had alarmed the opponents of slavery, who feared that the institution would extend indefinitely into the West. But by 1849–50, when the contest over the principle of the Wilmot Proviso was at its height, the western limits of the cotton-growing region were already approximated; and by the time the new Republican party was formed to check the further expansion of slavery, the westward march of the cotton plantation was evidently slowing down. The northern frontier of cotton production west of the Mississippi had already been established at about the northern line of Arkansas. Only a negligible amount of the staple was being grown in Missouri. West of Arkansas a little cotton was cultivated by the slaveholding, civilized Indians; but until the Indian territory should be opened generally to white settlement—a development of which there was no immediate prospect—it could not become a slaveholding region of any importance. The only possibility of a further westward extension of the cotton belt was in Texas. In that state alone was the frontier line of cotton and slavery still advancing.

In considering the possibilities of the further extension of slavery, then, it is necessary to examine the situation in Texas in the eighteen-fifties. Though slaves had been introduced into Texas by some of Stephen F. Austin's colonists, they were not brought in large numbers until after annexation. Before the Texas Revolution, the attitude of the Mexican government and the difficulty of marketing the products of slave labor had checked their introduction; while during the period of the Republic, the uncertainty as to the future of the country, the heavy tariff laid upon Texas cotton by the United States, which in the absence of a direct trade with Europe was virtually the only market for Texas cotton, and the low price of cotton after 1839, had been sufficient in general to restrain the cotton planter from emigrating to the new country. Annexation to the United States and the successful termination of the war with Mexico removed most of these impediments. Thereafter there was no tariff to pay; slave property was safe; land agents offered an abundance of cheap rich lands near enough to the coast and to navigable rivers to permit ready exportation; and the price of cotton was again at a profitable figure. Planters with their slaves poured into the new state in

increasing numbers. They settled along the northeastern
outlet by way of the Red River, or in the east and southea.
flowed into the Gulf. But these rivers were not navigable v
the planter who went far into the interior found difficulty in
market. He must either wait upon a rise in the river and depe
steamers or the risky method of floating his crop down on raft.
during the wet winter season along nearly impassable pioneer r
unbridged streams to Houston or Shreveport, or some other far-
his crop, the more time, difficulty, and expense of getting it to

Obviously, there was a geographic limit beyond which, under such conditions, the growth of large crops of cotton was unprofitable. Therefore, in the early fifties, the cotton plantations tended to cluster in the river counties in the eastern and southern parts of the state. While the small farmers and stockmen pushed steadily out into the central section of Texas, driving the Indians before them, the cotton plantations and the mass of the slaves lagged far behind. The up-country settlers grew their little crops of grain on some of the finest cotton lands of the world; and they sold their surplus to immigrants and to army posts. Few negroes were to be found on these upland farms, both because the prices demanded for slaves were too high for the farmers to buy them, and because the seasonal character of labor in grain growing rendered the use of slaves unprofitable. Though negro mechanics were in demand and were hired at high wages, the field hand had to be employed fairly steadily throughout the year if his labor was to show a profit. Negroes were even less useful in handling range stock than in farming and were rarely used for that purpose.

Therefore, the extension of the cotton plantation into the interior of Texas had to wait upon the development of a cheaper and more efficient means of transportation. As all attempts to improve the navigation of the shallow, snag-filled rivers failed, it became more and more evident that the only solution of the problem of the interior planter lay in the building of railroads. Throughout the eighteen-fifties, and indeed for two decades after the war, there was a feverish demand for railroads in all parts of the state. The newspapers of the period were full of projects and promises, and scores of railroad companies were organized or promoted. But capital was lacking and the roads were slow in building. Not a single railroad had reached the fertile black-land belt of central Texas by 1860. There can hardly be any question that the cotton plantations with their working forces of slaves would have followed the railroads westward until they reached the black-land prairies of central Texas or the semi-arid plains which cover the western half of the state. But would they have followed on into the prairies and the plains?

It is important to recall that eastern Texas, like the older South Atlantic and Gulf cotton region, is a wooded country, where the essential problem of enclosing fields was easily solved by the rail fence. But in the black-land prairies there was no fencing material, except for a little wood along the creeks; and during the fifties the small fields of the farmers were along these streams. The prairies, generally, were not enclosed and put under the plow until after the introduction of barbed wire in the late seventies. Unless the planter had resorted to the expense of shipping rails from eastern Texas, there was no way in which he could have made more use of the prairie lands than the

nd. Here, then, in the central black-land prairies, was a temporary barrier
to westward movement of the slave plantation. Beyond it was another barrier that
would have been permanently impassable.

Running north and south, just west of the black-land belt, and almost in the
geographical center of the state, is a hilly, wooded strip of varying width known as the
East and West Cross Timbers, which is prolonged to the south and southwest by the
Edwards Plateau. West of the Cross Timbers begins the semi-arid plain which rises to
the high, flat table-land of the Staked Plains, or Llano Estacado, in the extreme west and
northwest. Except for a few small cattle ranches, there were almost no settlements in
this plains country before 1860; and despite the heavy immigration into Texas after the
Civil War, it was not until the eighties that farmers began to penetrate this section.

The history of the agricultural development of the Texas plains region since 1880
affords abundant evidence that it would never have become suitable for plantation slave
labor. Let us turn, for a moment, to this later period. The Texas and Pacific Railroad,
completed by 1882 and followed by the building of other roads into and across the
plains, afforded transportation; and the introduction of barbed wire solved the fencing
problem. State and railroad lands were offered the settlers at low prices. Farmers began
moving into the eastern plains about 1880, but they were driven back again and again
by droughts. It took more than twenty years of experimentation and adaptation with
windmills, dry-farming, and new drought-resisting feed crops for the cotton farmer to
conquer the plains. There is little reason to believe that the conquest could have been
effected earlier; there is even less basis for belief that the region would ever have been
filled with plantations and slaves. For reasons which will be advanced later, it is likely
that the institution of slavery would have declined toward extinction in the Old South
before the cotton conquest of the plains could have been accomplished, even had there
been no Civil War. But if the institution had remained in full vigor elsewhere, it would
have been almost impossible to establish the plantation system in this semi-arid section
where, in the experimental period, complete losses of crops were so frequent. With so
much of his capital tied up in unremunerative laborers whom he must feed and clothe,
it is hard to see how any planter could have stayed in that country. Moreover, in the
later period the use of improved machinery, especially adapted to the plains, would have
made slave labor unnecessary and unbearably expensive. The character of the soil and
the infrequency of rainfall have enabled the western cotton farmer, since 1900, with the
use of this improved machinery to cultivate a far larger acreage in cotton, and other
crops as well, than was possible in the older South or in eastern Texas. The result has
been the appearance of a high peak in the demand for labor in western Texas in the
cotton-picking season. This has called for transient or seasonal labor as in the grain
fields—a situation that could not be met by the plantation system of slave labor. During
the last twenty-five years this section has become populous and prosperous; but the
beginning of its success as a cotton-growing region came fifty years after the Republican
party was organized to stop the westward advance of the "cotton barons" and their
slaves. It may or may not have any significance that the negro has moved but little
farther west in Texas than he was in 1860—he is still a rarity in the plains
country—although it may be presumed that his labor has been cheaper in freedom than
under slavery.

But let us look for a moment at the southwestern border of Texas. In 1860 slavery had stopped more than one hundred and fifty miles short of the Rio Grande. One obvious explanation of this fact is that the slaveowner feared to get too close to the boundary lest his bondmen escape into Mexico. There is no doubt that this fear existed, and that slaves occasionally made their way into that country. But it is worth noting that very little cotton was grown then or is yet grown on that border of Texas, except in the lower valley around Brownsville and along the coast about Corpus Christi. Other crops have proved better adapted to the soil and climate and have paid better. More significant still is the fact that very few negroes are found there today, for Mexican labor is cheaper than negro labor now, as it was in the eighteen-fifties. During the decade before secession, Mexican labor was used exclusively south of the Nueces River. After emancipation there was still no movement of negroes into the region where Mexican labor was employed. The disturbances which began in Mexico in 1910 have sent floods of Mexicans across the Rio Grande to labor in the fruit and truck farms of the valley and the cotton fields of south Texas. An interesting result is that the Mexican has steadily pushed the negro out of south Texas and to a considerable degree out of south-central Texas. Wherever the two have come into competition either on the farms or as day laborers in the towns, the Mexican has won. This would seem to show that there was little chance for the institution of African slavery to make headway in the direction of Mexico.

There was another situation which checked the extension of slavery into southwestern Texas. A large area of the most fertile lands had been settled by German immigrants, who had begun coming into that district in the late eighteen-forties. Not only were the Germans opposed to slavery; they were too poor to purchase slaves. They needed labor, as all pioneers do; but their needs were met by the steady inflow of new German immigrants, whose habit it was to hire themselves out until they were able to buy small farms for themselves. The system of agriculture of these industrious and frugal people had no place for the African, whether slave or free. Even today one sees few negroes among the original and typical German settlements. In 1860, east and southeast of San Antonio, these Germans formed a barrier across the front of the slaveholders. . . .

By the provisions of the Compromise of 1850, New Mexico, Utah, and the other territories acquired from Mexico were legally open to slavery. In view of well-known facts, it may hardly seem worthwhile to discuss the question whether slavery would ever have taken possession of that vast region; but perhaps some of those facts should be set down. The real western frontier of the cotton belt is still in Texas; for though cotton is grown in small quantities in New Mexico, Arizona, and California, in none of these states is the entire yield equal to that of certain single counties in Texas. In none is negro labor used to any appreciable extent, if at all. In New Mexico and Arizona, Mexican labor is cheaper than negro labor, as has been the case ever since the acquisition of the region from Mexico. It was well understood by sensible men, North and South, in 1850 that soil, climate, and native labor would form a perpetual bar to slavery in the vast territory then called New Mexico. Possibly southern California could have sustained slavery, but California had already decided that question for itself, and there was no remote probability that the decision would ever be reversed. As to New

Mexico, the census of 1860, ten years after the territory had been thrown open to slavery, showed not a single slave; and this was true, also, of both Colorado and Nevada. Utah, alone of all these territories, was credited with any slaves at all. Surely these results for the ten years when, it is alleged, the slave power was doing its utmost to extend its system into the West, ought to have confuted those who had called down frenzied curses upon the head of Daniel Webster for his Seventh-of-March speech.

At the very time when slavery was reaching its natural and impassable frontiers in Texas, there arose the fateful excitement over the Kansas-Nebraska Bill, or rather over the clause which abrogated the Missouri Compromise and left the determination of the status of slavery in the two territories to their own settlers. Every student of American history knows of the explosion produced in the North by the "Appeal of the Independent Democrats in Congress to the People of the United States," written and circulated by Senator Chase and other members of Congress. This fulmination predicted that the passage of the bill would result in debarring free home-seeking immigrants and laborers from a vast region larger, excluding California, than all the free states, and in converting it into a dreary waste filled with plantations and slaves. It was a remarkably skillful maneuver and it set the North, particularly the Northwest, on fire. But, in all candor, what of the truth of the prophecy? Can anyone who examines the matter objectively today say that there was any probability that slavery as an institution would ever have taken possession of either Kansas or Nebraska? Certainly cotton could not have been grown in either, for it was not grown in the adjacent part of Missouri. Hemp, and possibly tobacco, might have been grown in a limited portion of eastern Kansas along the Missouri and the lower Kansas rivers; and if no obstacle had been present, undoubtedly a few negroes would have been taken into eastern Kansas. But the infiltration of slaves would have been a slow process.

Apparently there was no expectation, even on the part of the pro-slavery men, that slavery would go into Nebraska. Only a small fraction of the territory was suited to any crops that could be grown with profit by slave labor, and by far the greater portion of Kansas—even of the eastern half that was available for immediate settlement—would have been occupied in a short time, as it was in fact, by a predominantly non-slaveholding and free-soil population. To say that the individual slaveowner would disregard his own economic interest and carry valuable property where it would entail loss merely for the sake of a doubtful political advantage seems a palpable absurdity. Indeed, competent students who have examined this subject have shown that the chief interest of the pro-slavery Missourians in seeking to control the organization of the territorial government was not so much in taking slaves into Kansas as in making sure that no free-soil territory should be organized on their border to endanger their property in western Missouri. They lost in the end, as they were bound to lose. The census of 1860 showed two slaves in Kansas and fifteen in Nebraska. In short, there is good reason to believe that had Douglas's bill passed Congress without protest, and had it been sustained by the people of the free states, slavery could not have taken permanent root in Kansas if the decision were left to the people of the territory itself. . . .

The agitation for the re-opening of the African slave trade is an interesting episode. Its proponents were a small group of extremists, mostly Secessionists, whose ostensible object was to cheapen the cost of labor for the small farmer who was too poor to pay the high prices for slaves that prevailed in the fifties. Another argument for re-opening the trade was that cheaper slave labor would enable the institution to extend its frontiers into regions where it was too expensive under existing conditions. Finally, the proponents of the movement insisted that unless the cost of slaves declined, the northern tier of slave states would be drained of their negroes until they themselves became free states, thus imperiling the security of the cotton states. There is some reason to suspect that their leaders designed to stir up the anti-slavery element in the North to greater hostility and to renewed attacks in the hope that the South would be driven into secession, which was the ultimate goal of this faction. These agitators were never able to commit a single state to the project, for not only did the border states condemn it but the majority of the people of the Gulf states also. Even Robert Barnwell Rhett, who was at first inclined to support the program, turned against it because he saw that it was dividing the state-rights faction and weakening the cause of southern unity. This in itself seems highly significant of the southern attitude.

If the conclusions that have been set forth are sound, by 1860 the institution of slavery had virtually reached its natural frontiers in the west. Beyond Texas and Missouri the way was closed. There was no reasonable ground for expectation that new lands could be acquired south of the United States into which slaves might be taken. There was, in brief, no further place for it to go. In the cold facts of the situation, there was no longer any basis for excited sectional controversy over slavery extension; but the public mind had so long been concerned with the debate that it could not see that the issue had ceased to have validity. In the existing state of the popular mind, therefore, there was still abundant opportunity for the politician to work to his own ends, to play upon prejudice and passion and fear. Blind leaders of the blind! Sowers of the wind, not seeing how near was the approaching harvest of the whirlwind!

Perhaps this paper should end at this point; but it may be useful to push the inquiry a little farther. If slavery could gain no more political territory, would it be able to hold what it had? Were there not clear indications that its area would soon begin to contract? Were there not even some evidences that a new set of conditions were arising within the South itself which would disintegrate the institution? Here, it must be confessed, one enters the field of speculation, which is always dangerous ground for the historian. But there were certain factors in the situation which can be clearly discerned, and it may serve some purpose to indicate them.

Reference has already been made to the increasingly high prices of slaves in the southwestern states throughout the eighteen-fifties. This price-boom was due in part to good prices for cotton; but though there had always previously been a fairly close correlation between cotton and slave prices, the peculiarity of this situation was that slave prices increased much faster than cotton prices from 1850 to the end of 1860. Probably the explanation lies in the abundance of cheap and fertile cotton lands that were available for planting in Louisiana, Arkansas, and Texas. Cheap lands enabled the planter to expand his plantation and to invest a relatively larger amount of his capital in slaves, and the continued good prices for cotton encouraged this expansion. These good prices for slaves were felt all the way back to the oldest slave states, where slave labor was less profitable, and had the effect of drawing away planters and slaves from Maryland, Virginia, North Carolina, Kentucky, and Missouri to the new Southwest.

This movement, to be sure, had been going on for several decades, but now the migration from the old border states was causing alarm among the pro-slavery men. Delaware was only nominally a slave state; Maryland's slave population was diminishing steadily. The ratio of slaves to whites was declining year by year in Virginia, Kentucky, and even in Missouri. The industrial revolution was reaching into these three states, and promised within less than another generation to reduce the economic interest in planting and slaveholding, as already in Maryland, to very small proportions.

The pro-slavery leaders in Virginia and Maryland endeavored to arrest this change by improving the condition of the planter. They renewed their efforts for a direct trade with Europe, and further stimulated interest in agricultural reforms. As already seen, the proponents of the revival of the African slave trade argued that cheaper slave labor in the lower South was necessary to prevent the border states from ultimately becoming free-soil. Though agricultural reform made headway, the other remedies failed to materialize; and the slow but constant transformation of the Atlantic border region proceeded. The greatest impediments were in the reluctance of the families of the old states, where slavery was strongly patriarchal, to part with their family servants, and in the social prestige which attached to the possession of an ample retinue of servants. It was evident, however, that the exodus would go on until the lure of the Southwest lost its force.

As long as there was an abundance of cheap and fertile cotton lands, as there was in Texas, and the prices of cotton remained good, there would be a heavy demand for labor on the new plantations. As far as fresh lands were concerned, this condition would last for some time, for the supply of lands in Texas alone was enormous. But at the end of the decade, there were unmistakable signs that a sharp decline in cotton prices and planting profits was close at hand. The production of cotton had increased slowly, with some fluctuations, from 1848 to 1857, and the price varied from about ten cents to over thirteen cents a pound on the New York market. But a rapid increase in production began in 1858 and the price declined. The crop of 1860 was twice that of 1850. Probably the increase in production was due in part to the rapid building of railroads throughout the South toward the end of the decade, which brought new lands within reach of markets and increased the cotton acreage; but part of the increase was due to the new fields in Texas. There was every indication of increased production and lower price levels for the future, even if large allowance be made for poor-crop years. There was small chance of reducing the acreage, for the cotton planter could not easily change to another crop. Had not the war intervened, there is every reason to believe that there would have been a continuous overproduction and very low prices throughout the sixties and seventies.

What would have happened then when the new lands of the Southwest had come into full production and the price of cotton had sunk to the point at which it could not be grown with profit on the millions of acres of poorer soils in the older sections? The replenishment of the soil would not have solved the problem for it would only have resulted in the production of more cotton. Even on the better lands the margin of profit would have declined. Prices of slaves must have dropped then, even in the Southwest;

importation from the border states would have fallen off; thousands of slaves would have become not only unprofitable but a heavy burden, the market for them gone. Those who are familiar with the history of cotton farming, cotton prices, and the depletion of the cotton lands since the Civil War will agree that this is no fanciful picture.

What would have been the effect of this upon the slaveowner's attitude toward emancipation? No preachments about the sacredness of the institution and of constitutional guarantees would have compensated him for the dwindling values of his lands and slaves and the increasing burden of his debts. It should not be forgotten that the final formulation and acceptance of the so-called pro-slavery philosophy belonged to a time when slaveowners, in general, were prosperous. With prosperity gone and slaves an increasingly unprofitable burden, year after year, can there be any doubt that thousands of slaveowners would have sought for some means of relief? How they might have solved the problem of getting out from under the burden without entire loss of the capital invested in their working force, it is hard to say; but that they would have changed their attitude toward the institution seems inevitable.

There was one difficulty about the problem of emancipation that has been little understood in the North, one that the Abolitionist refused to admit. It was the question of what to do with the freed negro. Could he take care of himself without becoming a public charge and a social danger? Would it not be necessary to get rid of the slave and the negro at the same time? But to get rid of the negro was manifestly impossible. Should he not then remain under some form of control both in his own interest and in the interest of the larger social order? There is some evidence that this problem was actually being worked out in those older states which had a large population of free negroes. In Virginia and Maryland, where the number of slaves on the plantation had been reduced in the interest of economy as improved farming machinery came into use, free negroes were coming to be relied upon when extra or seasonable labor was required. Though it is impossible to say how far this practice would have gone in substituting free-negro labor for slave labor, it would inevitably have accustomed increasing numbers of employers to the use of free negroes and have weakened by so much the economic interest in slavery. The cost of rearing a slave to the working age was considerable, and it is well within the probabilities that, in an era of over-stocked plantations and low cotton prices, the planter would have found that he was rearing slaves, as well as growing cotton, at a loss. New codes for the control of the free negroes might easily, in the course of time, have removed the greatest objection on the part of the nonslaveowners to emancipation.

In summary and conclusion: it seems evident that slavery had about reached its zenith by 1860 and must shortly have begun to decline, for the economic forces which had carried it into the region west of the Mississippi had about reached their maximum effectiveness. It could not go forward in any direction and it was losing ground along its northern border. A cumbersome and expensive system, it could show profits only as long as it could find plenty of rich land to cultivate and the world would take the product of its crude labor at a good price. It had reached its limits in both profits and lands. The free farmers in the North who dreaded its further spread had nothing to fear.

Even those who wished it destroyed had only to wait a little while—perhaps a generation, probably less. It was summarily destroyed at a frightful cost to the whole country and one third of the nation was impoverished for forty years. One is tempted at this point to reflections upon what has long passed for statesmanship on both sides of that long dead issue. But I have not the heart to indulge them.

twelve
the contradictory
nature of the
"natural limits"
thesis

EUGENE D. GENOVESE

*While challenging the economic reasoning in Ramsdell's article,
Professor Genovese points to the social and political needs of the planter
class as a factor in promoting slavery expansion. One should consider the
flaws in Ramsdell's thesis according to Genovese and the feasibility of
Genovese's proposal for slave labor in the Southwest and West. Genovese,
born May 19, 1930 in Brooklyn, New York, is a leading historian of
the antebellum South, as well as chairman of the history department at
the University of Rochester. He received his Ph.D. from Columbia
University (1959). Among his major works are* The Political
Economy of Slavery *(1965) and* The World the Slaveholders
Made *(1969).*

The "natural limits" thesis is self-contradictory—and, in one
important sense, irrelevant—for it simultaneously asserts that
slavery was nonexpansionist and that it would have perished
without room to expand. The only way to avoid judging the
thesis to be self-contradictory is to read it so as to state that
slavery needed room to expand but that, first, it needed room
only in the long run and, second, that it had no room. This
reading removes the contradiction but destroys the thesis.

Source: Eugene D. Genovese, *The Political Economy of Slavery* (New York: Alfred
A. Knopf, 1965), pp. 254–70. Footnotes omitted. Copyright © 1965 by Alfred A.
Knopf, Inc. Reprinted by permission of the publisher.

If the slave states would eventually need room to expand, they had to set aside new territory when they could get it or face a disaster in a few years or decades. Hence, wisdom dictated a fight for the right to take slaves into the territories, for ultimately that right would be transformed from an abstraction into a matter of life and death. W. Burwell of Virginia wrote in 1856 that the South needed no more territory at the moment and faced no immediate danger of a redundant slave population. "Yet statesmen," he concluded, "like provident farmers, look to the prospective demands of those who rely upon their forethought for protection and employment. Though, therefore, there may be no need of Southern territory for many years, yet it is important to provide for its acquisition when needed . . . ."

To establish that slavery had no room to expand is not to refute the theory of slavery expansionism. If it could be firmly established that slavery needed room to expand but had none, then we should have described a society entering a period of internal convulsion. The decision of most slaveholders to stake everything on a desperate gamble for a political independence that would have freed them to push their system southward emerges as a rational, if dangerous, course of action.

One of the most puzzling features of Ramsdell's essay is the virtual equation of cotton and slavery. Only occasionally and never carefully does he glance at the prospects for using slave labor outside the cotton fields. To identify any social system with a single commodity is indefensible, and in any case, Southern slavery had much greater flexibility. Ramsdell's essay is puzzling with respect to these general considerations but even more so with respect to his specific contention that contemporary Southerners viewed the territorial question as a cotton question. They did not.

When the more intelligent and informed Southerners demanded the West for slavery they often, perhaps most often, spoke of minerals, not cotton or even hemp. Slavery, from ancient times to modern, had proved itself splendidly adaptable to mining. Mining constituted one of the more important industries of the Negroes of preconquest Africa, and slave labor had a long history there. The Berbers, for example, used Negro slaves in West Africa, where the salt mines provided one of the great impetuses to the development of commerical, as opposed to traditional and patriarchal, forms of slavery. Closer in time and place to the South, Brazil afforded an impressive example of the successful use of slave labor in mining. In the middle of the eighteenth century diamond mining supplemented gold mining in Minas Gerais and accounted for a massive transfer of masters and slaves from the northeastern sugar region. Southern leaders knew a good deal about this experience. "The mines of Brazil," reported *De Bow's Review* in 1848, "are most prolific of iron, gold, and diamonds. . . . The operation is performed by negroes . . . 30,000 negroes have been so employed." The eastern slave states had had experience with gold mining, and although the results were mixed, the potentialities of slave labor had been demonstrated. Planters in the Southwestern states expressed interest in gold mines in Arkansas and hopefully looked further west. "If mines of such temporary value should, as they may, be found in the territories, and slaves could be excluded from these," wrote A. F. Hopkins of Mobile in 1860, "it would present a case of monstrous injustice."

During the Congressional debates of 1850, Representative Jacob Thompson of Mississippi, later to become Secretary of the Interior under Buchanan, expressed great concern over the fate of the public domain of California if it were to be hastily admitted to the Union and expressed special concern over the fate of the gold mines. Ten years later, after a decade of similar warnings, pleas, hopes, and threats, S. D. Moore of Alabama wrote that the South was "excluded from California, not pretendedly even by 'isothermal lines,' or want of employment for slave labor, for in regard to climate and mining purposes the country was admirably adapted to the institution of African slavery." Had it not been for the antislavery agitation, Representative Clingman told the House in 1850, Southerners would have used slaves in the mines of California and transformed it into a slave state. Albert Gallatin Brown, one of the most fiery and belligerent of the proslavery extremists, wrote his constituents that slave labor was admirably suited to mining and that California could and should be made into a slave state. Even as a free state California demonstrated the usefulness of slave labor. In 1852 the state legislature passed a mischievous fugitive slave law that could be and was interpreted to allow slaveholders to bring slaves into the state to work in the mines and then send them home.

Similarly, a Texan wrote in 1852 that a Mississippi and Pacific railroad would secure the New Mexico territory for the South by opening the mining districts to slave labor. During the War for Southern Independence, Jefferson Davis received a communication from his Southwestern field commander that a successful drive to California would add "the most valuable agriculture and grazing lands, and the richest mineral region in the world."

Southerners had long cast eyes toward Mexico and looked forward to additional annexations. "I want Cuba," roared Albert Gallatin Brown. "I want Tamaulipas, Potosí, and one or two other Mexican states; and I want them all for the same reason—for the planting or spreading of slavery." Throughout the 1850s, *De Bow's Review* printed articles about Mexico and particularly about Mexican mines. In 1846, Joel R. Poinsett reviewed Waddy Thompson's *Reflexions on Mexico* and noted the extensive mineral wealth in an article that struck no bellicose note. During the same year Gustavus Schmidt, in a humane, nonracist, nonchauvinist account, wrote of Mexico's "inexhaustible deposits of gold and silver." In 1850, Brantz Mayer of Baltimore estimated that one-fifth of Mexican territory contained excellent mineral resources. Covetous eyes and bellicose projects appeared soon enough.

The mineral resources of Mexico are unquestionably immense. . . . The moment Mexico falls into the hands of the Anglo-Saxon race, every inch of her territory will be explored. . . . The mines of Mexico, which have now been worked near three hundred years, are inexhaustible; and they only need the protection of a good government and the skill of an intelligent and industrious people, to render them productive of the most astonishing quantities of the precious metals.

George Frederick Holmes, in a long, rambling article on gold and silver mines, wrote glowingly of Chile as well as Mexico. H. Yoakum ended an article on Mexico with the warning, *"You must make progress, or you will be absorbed by a more energetic race."* Southerners and Mexicans took these designs seriously. Confederate troops marched into New Mexico with the intention of proceeding to Tucson and then swinging south to take Sonora, Chihuahua, Durango, and Tamaulipas. The Confederate government tried to deal with Santiago Vidaurri, the strong man of Coahuila and Nuevo León, to bring northern Mexico into the Confederacy, and Juárez was so alarmed that he was ready to go to great lengths to help the Union put down the rebellion.

It is one thing to note that Southerners sought to expand slavery into Mexico's mining districts or that they lamented the political barriers to the expansion of slavery into New Mexico's; it is another for us to conclude that their hopes and desires were more than wishful thinking. Allan Nevins has presented a formidable case to suggest that slavery had little room even in the mining districts of the Southwest and Mexico. He shows that even in the Gadsden Purchase the economic exigencies of mining brought about the quick suppression of the enterprising individual by the corporation. Western mining, as well as transportation, lumbering, and some forms of agriculture, required much capital and became fields for big business. High labor costs led to a rising demand for labor-saving machinery, but Nevins does not consider that this very condition might, under certain circumstances, have spurred the introduction of slave labor. He writes:

> *For three salient facts stood out in any survey of the Far West. First, this land of plain and peak was natural soil for a free-spirited and highly competitive society, demanding of every resident skill and intelligence. It was, therefore, even in that Gadsden Purchase country which had been bought at the behest of the slave states, a country naturally inhospitable to slavery. Second, when so much energy was steadily flowing into western expansion, and such wide outlets for more effort existed there, it was impossible to think of the country turning to Caribbean areas for a heavy thrust southward. Its main forces moved naturally toward the sunset, where rich opportunities were hardly yet sampled. The cotton kingdom, which realized that the West gave little scope for its peculiar culture, might plan grandiose Latin American adventures; but it would get little support from other regions. And in the third place, conditions in the West demanded capital and organization on a broad scale; if it was a land for individualists, it was even more a land for corporate enterprise—a land for the businessman. Those who pondered these three facts could see that they held an ominous meaning for the South. The nearer Northwest had already done much to upset the old sectional balance, and the Far West, as it filled up, would do still more.*

On economic grounds Nevins's analysis has much to offer, but his remarks on the competitive struggle in the Southwest and on the inability of Southerners to get national support for Caribbean adventures do not prove nearly so much as he thinks. At most, they suggest that the North was strong enough to block slavery expansionism into the Southwest and frustrate Southern ambitions elsewhere. If so, the case for secession, from the proslavery viewpoint, was unanswerable.

Nevins's remarks illustrate the wisdom of other Southern arguments—that the South had to secure new land politically, not by economic advance, and that the South had to have guarantees of positive federal protection for slavery in the territories. The *Charleston Mercury*, climaxing a decade of Southern complaints, insisted in 1860 that slavery would have triumphed in California's gold-mining areas if Southerners had had assurances of protection for their property. It singled out the mineral wealth of New Mexico as beckoning the South and even saw possibilities for slave-worked mining in Kansas. With fewer exaggerations De Bow, a decade earlier, had pointed to the political aspect of the problem: "Such is the strength and power of the Northern opposition that property, which is ever timid, and will seek no hazards, is excluded from the country in the person of the slave, and Southerners are forced, willingly or not, to remain at home. Emigrants, meanwhile, crowd from the North." During the bitter debate in Congress over the admission of California, Senator Jeremiah Clemens of Alabama replied heatedly to Clay in words similar to those used by De Bow. Free-soil agitation, he said, had kept slavery from the territories. "Property is proverbially timid. The slaveholder would not carry his property there with a threat hanging over him that it was to be taken away by operation of law the moment he landed." Representative Joseph M. Root of Ohio, Whig and later Republican, commented on such charges by boasting that if the Wilmot Proviso had accomplished nothing more than to create a political climate inimical to slavery expansion, it had accomplished its purpose.

The Southern demand for federal guarantees made sense, but even that did not go far enough. Ultimately, the South needed not equal protection for slave property but complete political control. If a given territory could be organized by a proslavery party, then slaveholders would feel free to migrate. Time would be needed to allow the slave population to catch up; meanwhile, free-soil farmers had to be kept out in favor of men who looked forward to becoming slaveholders. Under such circumstances the territory's population might grow very slowly, and the exploitation of its resources might lag far behind that of the free territories. Nothing essential would be lost to the South by underdevelopment; the South as a whole was underdeveloped. In short, the question of political power necessarily had priority over the strictly economic questions.

Even if the South had looked forward to extending the cotton kingdom, the political question would have had to take priority. Douglass C. North has incisively described the rhythm of such extensions:

> Long swings in the price of cotton were the result of periods of excess capacity with a consequent elastic supply curve of cotton over a substantial range of output. Once demand had shifted to the right sufficiently to use all available cotton land, the supply curve became rather inelastic. A rise in cotton prices precipitated another move into new lands of the Southwest by planters and their slaves. Funds from the Northeast and England financed the transfer of slaves, purchase of land, and working capital during the period of clearing the land, preparing the soil and raising a cotton crop. There was a lag of approximately four or five years between the initial surge and the resulting large increase in output which caused a tremendous shift to the right in the supply curve and the beginning of another lengthy period of digesting the increased capacity.

Under such circumstances the political safety of slavery, especially during the difficult interlude North describes, always had to be assured before any significant economic advance could occur. Significantly, even the long-range possibility of irrigating the Southwest was noted in *De Bow's Review* as early as 1848.

Slavery certainly would have had a difficult time in Kansas, although as Nevins has shown, greater possibilities existed than Stephen Douglas or many historians since have been prepared to admit. The proslavery leaders there, Atchison and Stringfellow, fully appreciated the importance of the prior establishment of political power, as their rough tactics and ingenious scheme to monopolize the timber and water resources showed. Nevins, on the other hand, questions the ability of the South to provide settlers. We shall return to this objection.

For the moment let us consider Kansas as solely and inevitably a wheat state. Large slave plantations have not proved well adapted to wheat growing, but small plantations were doing well in the Virginia tidewater. In open competition with Northwestern farmers the slaveholders probably would have been hurt badly. They knew as much. When, for example, Percy Roberts of Mississippi maintained that Negro slavery could thrive in the Northwest grain belt, he simultaneously maintained that the African slave trade would have to be reopened to drive down the cost of labor and put the slaveholders in a favorable competitive position. Historians like Nevins and Paul W. Gates have expressed confidence that slavery could not have triumphed in Kansas even if it had been allowed a foothold. They may be right, but only if one assumes that the South remained in the Union. Slavery expansionism required fastening proslavery regimes in such territories, but ultimately it required secession to protect the gains. Had Kansas joined a Southern Confederacy as a slave state, its wheat-growing slaveholders could have secured the same internal advantages as the sugar planters of Louisiana, and Union wheat could effectively have been placed at a competitive disadvantage in the Southern market.

Ramsdell's dismissal of Southern interest in Cuba and Central America, however necessary for his argument, does not bear examination. Southern sugar planters, who might have been expected to fear the glutting of the sugar market should Cuba enter the Union, spoke out for annexation. They seem to have been convinced that suspension of the African slave trade to Cuba would raise the cost of production there to American levels and that they would be able to buy Cuban slaves cheaply. Besides, as Basil Rauch points out, Louisiana sugar planters were moving to Cuba during the 1850s and looking forward to extending their fortunes. Southerners, like Northerners, often spoke of annexation in nationalist terms and sometimes went to great lengths to avoid the slavery question. J. J. Ampère heard that Cuba had been detached from the mainland by the Gulf Stream and rightfully belonged to the United States. He recommended that France reclaim Britain on the same grounds. He also heard that Cuba had to be annexed to provide a rest home for American consumptives. J. C. Reynolds, writing in *De Bow's Review* in 1850, described appalling losses in the illegal slave trade to Cuba and urged annexation to bring American law enforcement there and to end the terrible treatment of the Negroes. More sweepingly, some argued that without more territory the Negroes of the United States would be extinguished by overpopulation and attendant famine. All for the poor Negroes! Others, like Soulé and Albert Gallatin Brown, bluntly demanded Cuba and Central America to strengthen and defend slavery.

As for William Walker, he said enough to refute the Scroggs-Ramsdell interpretation. His *War in Nicaragua* makes clear that American politics made it necessary for him to appear to renounce annexation and that he was biding his time. No matter. His purpose there, as he boldly proclaimed, was to expand slavery as a system.

Opposition to territorial expansion by many Southerners has led some historians to deny the existence of an "aggressive slaveocracy" or to assert, with Ramsdell, that Southerners were too individualistic to be mobilized for such political adventures, which were often contrary to their private interests. No conspiracy theory is required. That there were many Southern leaders who sensed the need for more territory and fought for it is indisputable. That individual Southerners were not always willing to move when the interests of their class and system required them to merely indicates one of the ways in which slavery expansionism proved a contradictory process. Southerners opposed expansion for a variety of reasons, but mostly because they feared more free states. Expansion southward had the great advantage of not being cotton expansion, and the economic argument against it was weak. On the other hand, many feared that the annexation of Cuba would provide an excuse for the annexation of Canada or that the annexation of Mexico would repeat the experience of California. This opposition should be understood essentially as a preference for delaying expansion until secession had been effected, although there were, of course, many who opposed both.

If the slave South had to expand to survive, it paradoxically could not do so when given the opportunity. Unsettled political conditions prevented the immigration of slave property, much as the threat of nationalization or of a left-wing or nationalist coup prevents the flow of American capital to some underdeveloped countries to which it is invited.

"Where," asks Allan Nevins when discussing Kansas, "were proslavery settlers to come from? Arkansas, Texas, and New Mexico were all calling for slaveholding immigrants, and the two first were more attractive to Southerners than Kansas." Slave property necessarily moved cautiously and slowly. So long as it had to move at the pace set by Northern farmers, it would be defeated. The mere fact of competition discouraged the movement of slaveholders, and if they were willing to move, they could not hope to carry enough whites to win.

An area could be safely absorbed by the slave regime only by preventing Northern free-soilers from entering. Danhof has demonstrated that farm making was an expensive business. Northern farmers had a hard time; Southern farmers, without slaves or minimal savings, found it much harder. Traditionally, the more energetic nonslaveholders moved into new land first and cleared it; the planters followed much later. If those early settlers had to secure the territory against free-soilism before the planters and slaveholders moved in, the struggle could not ordinarily be won. Many Southern nonslaveholders could be and were converted to the antislavery banner once they found themselves away from the power and influence of the slaveholders. Charles Robinson bitterly criticized John Brown for his inability to appreciate the possibilities of persuasion: "While our free state colonies were trying to convert the whites from the South and make them sound free-state men, John Brown thought it better to murder them."

Missouri and Kansas, therefore, were worlds apart. W. A. Seay, in an article entitled "Missouri Safe for the South," dismissed suggestions that Missouri would abolish slavery. The nonslaveholding counties, he noted, lay in the southern part of the state and were inhabited by men from other parts of the South who owned no slaves only because they were as yet too poor. Their allegiance to the system rested ultimately on the ability of the slaveholders to retain political power and social and ideological leadership and to prevent these men of the lower classes from seeing an alternative way of life. Yet, by 1860 even Missouri had become a battleground because of its special geographic position and Northern and foreign immigration. Kansas could never be secured for slavery unless the slaveholders had political control and the migrating Southern farmers were isolated from corrupting influences. As it was, Northerners, according to Representative William Barksdale of Mississippi, went as families, whereas Southerners often went as young adventurers who had no intention of remaining once the excitement was over.

The South's anguish arose from having to expand and being unable to meet the tests of expansion set by life in mid-nineteenth-century America. Like T. S. Eliot's Hollow Men, it found that

Between the desire
And the spasm
Between the potency
And the existence
Between the essence
And the descent
Falls the shadow

Only if a territory shut out free-soil immigration, quickly established the political hegemony of the slaveholders, and prepared for a much slower development than Northerners might give it, could it be secured for slavery. These conditions negated slavery expansionism, but only so long as the South remained in the Union.

The South had to expand, and its leaders knew it. "There is not a slaveholder in this House or out of it," Judge Warner of Georgia declared in the House of Representatives in 1856, "but who knows perfectly well that whenever slavery is confined within certain specified limits, its future existence is doomed." The Republican party, said an editorial in *The Plantation* in 1860, denies that it wants to war on slavery, but it admits that it wants to surround it with free states. To do so would be to crush slavery where it now exists. Percy L. Rainwater's study of sentiment in Mississippi in the 1850s shows how firmly convinced slaveholders were that the system had to expand or die. Lincoln made the same point in his own way. He opposed any compromise on slavery expansion in 1860 because he feared new and bolder expansionist schemes and because he wished to contain slavery in order to guarantee its ultimate extinction.

Nevins's discussion of Lincoln's view illuminates one of the most tenacious and dubious assumptions on which many historians have based their interpretations of the origins of the war:

In view of all the trends of nineteenth century civilization, the terrible problem of
slavery could be given a final solution only upon the principle . . . of gradual
emancipation. . . . The first step was to stop the expansion of slavery, and to confine

*the institution within the fifteen states it already possessed. Such a decision would be
equivalent to a decree that slavery was marked for gradual evolution into a higher
labor system. Slavery confined would be slavery under sentence of slow death. The
second step would be the termination of slavery in the border states. Missouri by 1859
stood near the verge of emancipation . . .*

The assumption on which these notions rest is that the South, faced with containment,
could have accepted its consequences. On the further assumption that men may agree to
commit suicide, the assumption is plausible.

If instead of speaking of the South or of the system of slavery, we speak of the
slaveholders who ruled both, the assumption is less plausible. The extinction of slavery
would have broken the power of the slaveholders in general and the planters in
particular. Ideologically, these men had committed themselves to slaveholding and the
plantation regime as the proper foundations of civilization. Politically, the preservation
of their power depended on the preservation of its economic base. Economically, the
plantation system would have tottered under free labor conditions and would have
existed under some intermediary form like sharecropping only at the expense of the old
ruling class. The "higher" forms depended on the introduction of commercial relations
that would have gradually undermined the planters and guaranteed the penetration of
outside capital. We have the postbellum experience to cite here, although it took place
at a time when the planters had suffered hard blows, but slaveholders saw the dangers
before the war and before the blows. "Python," in a series of brilliant articles in
De Bow's Review in 1860, warned that emancipation, even with some form of
"apprenticeship" for the Negroes, would open the way for Northern capital to
command the productive power of the South. Once Negro labor is linked to capital in
the open market, he argued, rather than through the patriarchal system of plantation
slavery, it will fall prey to a predatory, soulless, Northern capitalism. There will be no
place left for the old master class, which will be crushed by the superior force of
Northern capital and enterprise or absorbed into them. "Of what advantage is it to the
South," he asked, "to be destroyed by Mr. Douglas through territorial sovereignty to
the exclusion of Southern institutions, rather than by Mr. Seward through
Congressional sovereignty to the same end? What difference is there to the South
whether they are forcibly led to immolation by Seward, or accorded, in the alternative,
the Roman privilege of selecting their own mode of death, by Douglas? Die they must
in either event."

These words demonstrate that the probable effect of a "higher labor system" on the
fortunes of the slaveholding class was not beyond the appreciation of its intellectual
leaders. We need not try to prove that so specific an appreciation was general. The
slaveholders knew their own power and could not help being suspicious of sweeping
changes in their way of life, no matter how persuasively advanced. Their slaveholding
psychology, habit of command, race pride, rural lordship, aristocratic pretensions,
political domination, and economic strength militated in defense of the status quo.
Under such circumstances an occasional voice warning that a conversion to tenantry or
sharecropping carried serious dangers to their material interests sufficed to stiffen their
resistance.

No demagogy or dogmatic speculation produced "Python's" fears. Even modest compensation—paid for by whom?—would have left the planters in a precarious position. At best, it would have extended their life as a class a little while longer than postbellum conditions permitted, but Northern capital could not long be kept from establishing direct relationships with tenants and sharecroppers. The planters would have steadily been reduced to middlemen of doubtful economic value or would have merged imperceptibly into a national business class. The change would have required, and eventually did require under disorderly postbellum conditions, extensive advances to laborers in the form of additional implements, fertilizer, household utensils, even food, and innumerable incidentals. This process guaranteed the disintegration of the old landowning class, however good an adjustment many of its members might have made to the new order.

Those who, like Max Weber, Ramsdell, even Phillips, and countless others, assume that the South could have accepted a peaceful transition to free labor gravely misjudge the character of its ruling class. The question of such a judgment is precisely what is at issue. . . . A revisionist historian might accept the empirical findings reported here and even the specific interpretations of their economic significance and still draw different conclusions on the larger issues. The final set of conclusions, and the notion of a general crisis itself, eventually must rest on agreement that the slaveholders constituted a ruling class and that they displayed an ideology and psychology such as has merely been suggested in these studies.

The slaveholders, not the South, held the power to accede or resist. To these men slaves were a source of power, pride, and prestige, a duty and a responsibility, a privilege and a trust; slavery was the foundation of a special civilization imprinted with their own character. The defense of slavery, to them, meant the defense of their honor and dignity, which they saw as the essence of life. They could never agree to renounce the foundation of their power and moral sensibility and to undergo a metamorphosis into a class the nature and values of which were an inversion of their own. Slavery represented the cornerstone of their way of life, and life to them meant an honor and dignity associated with the power of command. When the slaveholders rose in insurrection, they knew what they were about: in the fullest sense, they were fighting for their lives.

thirteen political movement for industrial slavery in the south

ROBERT S. STAROBIN

Robert S. Starobin (1939–1971) received his Ph.D. from the University of California at Berkeley (1968) and had taught at the University of Wisconsin and the State University of New York at Binghamton. Among his publications are Slavery As It Was *(1971) and* Denmark Vesey: The Slave Conspiracy of 1822 *(1970). Starobin, in this selection, argues that the campaign for slave-based industries merged with growing Southern nationalism into a movement for Southern secession.*

Industrial leaders also grappled with the knottiest issue of the 1840's and 1850's—territorial and economic expansionism. Southern expansionism stemmed from many causes—specifically, soil exhaustion in the seaboard slave states, the waning of southern political power, the desire to establish "buffer zones" against hostile political and economic concentrations in the free states and elsewhere, and the need to provide land for restless, pushy, and grasping slaveowners and yeoman farmers. But some Southerners also assumed—as Eugene Genovese has pointed out—that expansion would enable them to use slave labor in mining and sugar milling in Mexico and the Caribbean. Other

Source: Robert S. Starobin, *Industrial Slavery in the Old South* (New York: Oxford University Press, 1970), pp. 214–22, 228–32. Footnotes omitted. Copyright © 1970 by Oxford University Press, Inc. Reprinted by permission of the publisher.

113

businessmen were more interested in using slave labor in mining, lumbering, and transportation enterprises in the American West. A direct relationship therefore existed between the industrial uses of slave labor and southern expansionism.

Southerners had long desired to use slaves in western mining ventures. In the early 1810's, Southerners pressured the Illinois Territory into permitting the use of slaves in the salt mines at Shawneetown. Illinois residents and Southerners alike reasoned that Negroes were better suited than white men to withstand salt mine labor. Thus, slaves were eventually allowed, with their masters' consent, to enter Illinois and "to hire themselves out" at the salines on an annual basis. Upon the bondsmen's return home, the masters received most of the "wages." Illinois also adopted "indenture" laws permitting slaveowners to bring their slaves into the territory under lifetime contracts. Largely the work of former Southerners, these laws and practices met little objection from a federal government directed by southern Presidents.

In the 1820's, when gold was discovered in the southern Piedmont, slaveowning Carolinians and Georgians attempted time and again to abrogate federal treaties protecting Indian lands to the west. Despite federal prohibitions, slaveowners illegally entered the Cherokee Territory and began digging gold. ". . . My worthy friend," begged one miner to President Andrew Jackson, "the object of this letter is to crave your friendly permission for myself to dig for Gold in the Cherokee Country. I have three sons and as many son in laws living not far distant from me," the slaveowner stated, "and we can spare among us forty strong and active [black] hands and still retain a force sufficient to make our bread, and that is all we can do in a country like ours where we cannot grow Cotton or Tobacco. . . ." By 1835, slaveowning miners had occupied Indian lands, while the Cherokees were being prodded along the "Trail of Tears."

By the late 1840's, Southerners were anxious to work mines in Mexican territories and to keep the gold, silver, copper, and rock mines of California, New Mexico, and Utah within slave territories or states. Along with other "forty-niners" slaveowners came to California seeking wealth, and, by 1850, several hundred slaves were already at work in the gold mining districts. Since many whites considered slave labor unfair competition, especially after some bondsmen helped their masters strike it rich, slavery became an important issue in early California politics. The slavery expansion issue surfaced at the California constitutional convention of 1849, where it was, along with the related issue of Negro exclusion, the chief topic of debate. Several delegates said they had received letters from slaveowners inquiring about the attitude toward bondage in California and declaring their intention of emigrating if their property could be assured of protection. Others argued against slavery because it could out-compete free labor and would eventually leave a residue of free blacks in the state. In the end, the convention unanimously prohibited slavery and barely defeated Negro exclusion.

The relationship between southern expansionism and slave-based mining was also manifest during the congressional debates of 1849–50 over the status of California. "I hold that the pursuit of gold-washing and mining is better adapted to slave labor than to any other species of labor recognized among us," declared Jefferson Davis. Another Mississippi representative feared that California's gold mines would be seized by Free Soilers and lost to the South; Representative Albert Gallatin Brown reiterated to his

Mississippi constituents that slave labor was so admirably suited to mining that California should be made a slave state. In spite of such rhetoric, California entered the Union in 1850 as a free state.

The exclusion of slavery from California did not prevent its continued existence in the state after 1850, however. White settlers did not demand the strict enforcement of prohibition and many slaves were unaware that they could claim their freedom. More important, Southerners made further attempts to introduce slavery as late as 1851, when over twelve hundred citizens of South Carolina and Florida petitioned the California Legislature for permission to settle in the state with their slaves. Similarly, James Gadsden, the former president of the slaveowning South Carolina Railroad and the soon-to-be minister to Mexico, attempted to found a slaveowning colony in California. "I was much disappointed at not having read the result of my Memorial to Your Legislature," Gadsden confided to Thomas Jefferson Green, a Southerner who had earlier mined gold in California with his slaves and then become a state legislator. "But if it is responded to favourably You may rest assured it will be the stimulating basis for the Organization of a Colony under my lead, . . . a colony which is to be the basis and stimulating influences to the permanent & future prosperity of California—Negro Slavery under Educated & Intelligent Masters can alone accomplish this," Gadsden continued. "They have been the Pioneers & basis of the civilization of Savage Countries—Without an enduring & well regulated labor the agricultural resources of the Pacific will never be developed—and a profitable agriculture is the foundation of a nations prosperity, happiness & wealth—The Mines may & will prove powerful auxiliaries: & combined with the Cultivation of the Soil must make California all that the Most Sanguine & Even Romantic have pictured. . . . So I am in Earnest if you only make the grants. . . ." Though such ambitions came to naught, slavery expansion still remained a political issue in California until the late 1850's.

Free-soil congressmen were aware of southern schemes to capture western mines for slavery. "As to California, I am equally clear," responded Oregon's well-traveled congressional delegate to a query by Horace Mann of Massachusetts. "California will always be a mining country, and wages will range high. At present slave labor in California would be . . . profitable. . . . And I have always been of the opinion, that wherever there is a mining country, if not in a climate uncongenial to slave labor, that species of labor would be profitable. That it would be in California mines, is evident. That these whole regions are filled with rich mines, is little less than certain, and that they can be run with slave labor is sure. Hence, were I a southern man and my property invested in slaves," he concluded, "I should consider the markets of New Mexico, Utah, and California, for slave labor, worthy of an honorable contest to secure." Mann himself surmised that "mines are the favorite sphere for slavery, as the ocean is for commerce."

The loss of the gold mines when California became a free state severely shocked many Southerners. At the Nashville disunion convention of 1850, for example, it was resolved that "California is peculiarly adapted for slave labor." Mississippi's Governor John A. Quitman, the slaveowning woodyard operator, cried to a special legislative session in 1850:

. . . The value of slaves depends upon the demand for their labor. The history of the cultivation of our great staples shows that this value is permanently enhanced by the

*opening of new fields of labor. The immense profits which have and still continue to
reward well directed industry in the gold mines of California, exceed those which have
ever flowed from mere labor, inexhaustible in extent and indefinite in duration. Had
this wide field for investment been open to the slave labor of the Southern States, wages
would have risen, and consequently the value of slaves at home would have been
greatly enhanced. Many hundreds of millions of dollars would have been added to the
capital of the Southern States . . . These estimates of pecuniary interest . . . are
founded upon the fixed opinion of almost every well informed person among us. . . .*

If free-soil agitators had not interfered, complained a North Carolina congressman in
1850, Southerners would have been able to work the gold mines of California with their
slaves and they would soon have secured it as a slave state.

Throughout the last antebellum decade, Southerners mourned the loss of western
mines. "We said, three years ago, in a public journal," wailed the Richmond *Dispatch* in
1852, "that California would be sure to remove every restriction that could be placed
upon her by the general government; and that she would be the largest slaveholder of
all the States. The thing seemed to us so palpable that we could not see how any man
could doubt it. What makes Louisiana and Texas such large slaveholders?" asked the
Dispatch. "—Why, the remuneration received for slave labor. What makes any country
a slaveholding country? The prospect of gain. And where can slave labor be so
profitably employed as in the gold mines of California? . . . The only way to develop
the resources of a piece of gold property belonging to an individual," concluded the
editor, "is to employ slaves." "I want Cuba, I want Tamaulipas, Potosi, and one or two
other Mexican [mining] states," raged Mississippi's Albert Gallatin Brown in 1858,
"and I want them all for the same reason—for the planting or spreading of slavery." If
slaves were excluded from territorial mines, moaned a Mobile citizen, as late as 1860, "it
would present a case of monstrous injustice." Pointing to the mineral wealth in New
Mexico, Arizona, and even, potentially, Kansas, the Charleston *Mercury* concluded:
"The right to have property protected in the territory is not a mere abstraction without
application or practical value. . . . When gold mines were discovered, slaveholders at
the South saw that, with their command of labor, it would be easy at a moderate outlay
to make fortunes digging gold. . . . There is no vocation in the world in which slavery
can be more useful and profitable than in mining."

Southerners also promoted expansionism to be able to use slave labor in western
lumbering and in Caribbean sugar milling enterprises. ". . . There are many more
places [besides western Florida and southern Alabama] where [saw] mills may be
erected very advantageously—" confided one Carolinian to another in 1854. "You have
the facts as they have been told me and you can judge of the results. I have no doubt
. . . that more money can be made in this business [cypress and juniper lumbering and
sawmilling] than any other when [slave] manual labor is used in the S. West."
Southern sugar millers frequently advocated the annexation of Cuba, despite fears of
glutted markets. In the 1850's, some Louisiana planters even moved to Cuba to invest in
sugar milling; they also realized that Cuban sugar production would complement that
of the slave states and that Cuban blacks could be brought to the mainland to work. In

any event, seizing Cuba and the Southwest would strengthen the political power of the slave states.

For much the same ends southern expansionists also proposed to construct transcontinental railroads with slave labor. Southwestern lines would tap the Pacific Coast and Oriental trade for southern merchants and cities, and, according to one Texan, a "Mississippi and Pacific" railroad would turn the western territories into slave states by making mining districts accessible to slave labor. "Now as to the route," wrote James Gadsden in 1851 concerning a railroad to a California slave colony, "I shall go by land & endeavor to be the pioneer on the Route I indicated for a Railroad. . . . I should like to know . . . whether Vehicles can descend the valley of the Gehela. . . . We will . . . make our Road as we go by an organized Corps of Pioneers & Axe men & reach California with both Negroes and animals in full vigor to go to work. . . . The neighbourhood of San Diego has presented attractions—& the Mouth of the Colorado with the Gila: an imposing Point," concluded Gadsden. "That Point if accessible would control the Gulf of California."

By the mid-1850's, the United States had acquired the Gila River valley with Gadsden's Purchase, Secretary of War Jefferson Davis had surveyed a southerly transcontinental route, and southern expansionists had begun to construct this railroad through Texas with slave labor. "A considerable amount of the companies Lands along the line of the road may be settled with the old [,] the youth & females [slaves belong to the company]," wrote Thomas Jefferson Green to the Southern Pacific Railroad's executive committee, of which he was a member, in 1856. "A considerable number of hands (negroes) are at work on this road [The Southern Pacific]," a prominent Texas physician reminded his legislature the same year. "The importance of pushing forward the construction of this road cannot be overestimated for the South. Being built by slave labor it insures a tier of slaveholding States along its line to the Pacific Ocean." . . .

In the late 1850's, as southern nationalism intensified, secessionists increasingly championed the employment of slave labor to help create southern industries. "Slave labor is certain to enable the South to manufacture so as to undersell the rest of the world," editorialized the New Orleans *Picayune* in 1858. A year later, another secessionist painted this picture of southern independence for a group of Georgians interested in reviving the slave trade:

If the South would but . . . shake off those restrictions that cramp her energies, a bright future awaits her. Her rich valleys will be cultivated, her streams bridged and her rivers levied, her plains traversed by Railroads, and dotted with villages. . . . Her forests will be disturbed by the sound of the woodman's axe, accompanied by the hum of the factory and the shrill snort of the locomotive. In short, she would be what she ought to be, a progressive, prosperous and powerful country, able to command respect in the Union, or if need be, defend herself out of it.

"We think it rigidly demonstrable," wrote "Washington City" to *De Bow's Review* in May, 1860, "that the ultimate result of disunion would be to give increased activity and impetus to every branch of Southern industry."

The relationships between disunion and slave-based industry were also expressed by many slaveowning manufacturers who became secessionists in the 1850's and supporters of the Confederacy in the 1860's. Georgia's Governor Charles J. McDonald, a slaveowning textile manufacturer, joined the pro-secession faction of the Nashville disunion convention as early as 1850. Duff Green, the famous industrial promoter, was devoted first to John C. Calhoun and later to southern nationhood. Henry W. Collier, a leading Alabama cotton miller, preached moderation as Governor from 1849 to 1853, but he joined William Lowndes Yancey's secessionist faction by the end of the 1850's. Robert L. Caruthers, a prominent Tennessee textile manufacturer, likewise shifted from early unionism in time to be chosen a confederate governor in 1861.

Similarly, William W. Harlee, president of the slave-employing Wilmington and Manchester Railroad, voted for immediate secession at the South Carolina disunion convention in December, 1860. Mark A. Cooper, a leading Georgia iron manufacturer, became an ardent advocate of southern economic independence. Joseph Reid Anderson, president of the slaveowning Tredegar Iron Works of Richmond, Virginia, eagerly became the "Ironmaker to the Confederacy." And Barrington King, a slaveowning Georgia textile miller, privately confided during the height of the secession crisis that "unless that abolition spirit is put down in the north, our only safety is to form a Southern Confederacy. . . . Water and oil cannot be united."

Most southern industrialists may have been cautious about disunion or politically inactive, but many of them were in the forefront of southern nationalism. For the evidence indicates that those industrialists present at the secession conventions of 1860–61 were usually secessionists, either of the "immediatist" or "co-operationist" variety. Moreover, other industrialists, including William Gregg, Rufus L. Patterson, and Robert Jemison, Jr., to name but a few, signed their states' ordinances of secession and thereby lent their tacit support to the designs of the disunionists.

After secession, many slaveowning manufacturers who had only reluctantly acceded to disunion became active supporters of the Confederacy—indicating further the link between industrial slavery and southern nationalism. Rufus Barringer, the prominent North Carolina manufacturer became a famous rebel army general. The Bell-Yeatman family, which controlled one of the largest slaveowning iron works in middle Tennessee, became a staunch backer of southern nationhood. More than a score of other industrialists served in the Confederate Congress. Governor Francis W. Pickens, however, perhaps best summed up the sentiments of the secessionists in his November, 1861, message to the South Carolina Assembly. "True war is a great calamity," he wrote, "but if this war shall end, as there is every prospect that it will do, by making us not only independent of our most deadly enemies, but commercially independent also, and at the same time, shall develop our own artisan skill and mechanical labor, so as to place us entirely beyond their subsidy hereafter, then, indeed, will it prove, in the end, a public blessing."

By the time of secession in 1861, the use of slave labor to industrialize the South had become accepted in theory and practice. This movement—to "bring the cotton mills to the cotton fields," so to speak—did not begin suddenly in the 1840's or even in the 1880's, as some historians have suggested. Industries emerged at least as early as the 1790's, and the campaigns for industry became most intense when Southerners felt least secure within the Union. The greatest interest in slave-based industries thus occurred from the late 1820's to the early 1830's, when southern agriculture was in difficulty, the tariff controversy raged, and when the South was coming under intense moral criticism. Interest also developed during the late 1840's and 1850's, when anti-slavery parties emerged and the sectional conflict was most bitter.

By the time of the Civil War, the struggle for southern self-sufficiency had reached a climax. Slaveowning agriculturists were now vigorously campaigning for slave-based industrialization and they were investing some of their surplus capital in southern industries. Such men, who included many influential Southerners, had overcome their traditional agrarianism and whatever backward-looking tendencies they may have had. They were seeking to create a balanced economy in which the South's great natural potential for agriculture would be complemented by its opportunities for extracting, processing, manufacturing, and transporting its resources and staples. Indeed, one reason why they wanted to expand slavery into the territories, and if possible to reopen the African slave trade, was to accelerate the development of southern industries.

Slaveowners were determined to industrialize the South under their own auspices exclusively, however, so that existing class and caste relationships would remain unchanged. They therefore opposed the creation not only of a slaveless industrial bourgeoisie independent of planter control, but also of a free industrial labor force. Had either of these two groups come into being, it might have challenged the slaveowners' domination of southern society. Unless slaveowners directed industries themselves, their ultimate security as a class was in jeopardy.

To maintain their hegemony, slaveowners insisted that slaves continue to be the chief labor force in southern industries. Long experience had demonstrated that bondsmen were more tractable, efficient, and profitable than alternative labor forces. The proslavery ideology also dictated that slaves were less troublesome than whites and better suited to work in tropical climates. Slaveowners also stymied the challenges of poor whites and free artisans by permitting the former to work in some textile mills and the latter to compete with some slave craftsmen. Finally, slaveowning agriculturists insisted that they themselves, or their allies, should continue to control southern industries, in order to prevent the emergence of independent entrepreneurial groups. Industrialists hoped that by these arrangements caste conflicts would continue to subsume class conflicts and that slaveowners would remain the dominant class.

Industrially minded Southerners also came into conflict with their northern counterparts for various reasons. Since southern industries lagged behind those of the North and trading patterns seemed unfair, slave employers had great difficulty competing in market places. The use of slave labor in industries helped reduce these disadvantages, but it could not overcome lost time entirely. The political power of slaveowners within the Union also seemed threatened by outsiders, as the North's population increased, as the Abolitionist attack became more shrill, as more and more free states entered the Union, and especially as the Republican Party—dedicated at least to the containment of slavery in the states—gained ground.

As a result, by the 1850's, many Southerners felt frustrated so long as they remained within a hostile Union. They believed that economic self-sufficiency, territorial expansion, the continuance of slavery, and their political survival depended on southern independence and could only be achieved by disunion. Slave-based industrialization and slave-state nationalism had, by 1861, entwined in a bloody struggle for southern sovereignty. Industrial slavery had, in this sense, directly contributed to the coming of the Civil War.

part six
slavery
in the
americas

fourteen
latin american slavery:
human rights preserved

STANLEY ELKINS

In this selection Professor Elkins shows that Latin American slavery was much less harsh and restrictive than slavery in the United States. Separate and competing interests of the crown, the planter, and the Catholic church influenced this development. As has been accentuated by the previous articles, these forces did not operate in the United States. Refer to Elkins's first essay to note the differences (p. 49).

In the colonies of Latin America we are able to think of the church, the civil authority, and the property concerns of the planter-adventurer as constituting distinct and not always harmonious interests in society. The introduction of slaves into the colonies brought much discomfort to the royal conscience; when the trade in Negroes became of consequence, the monarchs gave it their growing concern, and it never occurred to them not to retain over it a heavy measure of royal control. Charles V, who had granted the first license to transport Negroes in quantity directly from Africa to America, turned against the principle late in his reign and ordered the freeing of all African slaves in

Source: Stanley Elkins, *Slavery: A Problem in American Institutional and Intellectual Life* (Chicago: University of Chicago Press, 1959), pp. 67–80. Copyright © 1959 by The University of Chicago. Footnotes omitted. Reprinted with permission.

Spanish America.* In 1570 King Sebastian of Portugal issued an order to the colonists
of Brazil which forbade the taking of slaves except by "licit means," specifying that in
any case they must be registered within two months or all authority over them be
forfeited. A century later it had become clear to the monarchs of Spain that both the
demands of their colonists for labor and the revenue needs of the royal treasury required
that the trade in African Negroes be accorded full legitimacy. But the king in 1679 still
had to be assured "whether meetings of theologians and jurists have been held to
determine whether it is licit to buy them as slaves and make asientos for them and
whether there are any authors who have written on this particular question." Again we
find the king of Spain, in a *Real Cedula* of 1693, commanding the captain-general of
Cuba to call upon all masters of slaves, and to "say to them in my name that they must
not, for whatever motive, rigorously tighten the wage they receive from their slaves, for
having been tried in other places, it has proved inconvenient harming the souls of these
people.ᵥ . . ." Since slavery was "a sufficient sorrow without at the same time suffering
the distempered rigor of their master," any excesses were to be punished by applying
"the necessary remedy." The monarchy made terms when it met with the full force of
this new enterprise—new at least with respect to its proportions. But the energy with
which it imposed its own terms was drawn both from the ancient sanctions regarding
servitude and from the traditional force of the crown's institutional prerogatives.

The other item in this equation was the presence of a powerful church with needs of
its own. A considerable measure of its power as an institution naturally depended upon
its position of leadership in matters touching the morals of society. The maintenance of
that leadership required the church as a matter of course to insist on a dominant role in
the formulation of all policy which might bear on the morality of the slave system and
have consequences for the Faith. The terms it made with slavery paralleled those made
by the crown and exhibited the same ambiguities. In effect, the church with one hand
condemned slavery and with the other came to an understanding with it as a labor
system. Its doctrine asserted in general that the practice of slavery and the slave trade
was fraught with perils for those of the faithful who engaged in it and that they stood,
at innumerable points, in danger of mortal sin. The immoralities connected with the
trade compelled again and again the attention of church writers, and it was in this sense
that the Franciscan Father Thomas Mercado had denounced it in 1587 as fostering "two
thousand falsehoods, a thousand robberies, and a thousand deceptions." More
temperately summarizing the most learned opinion of his age, Germain Fromageau, a
doctor of the Sorbonne, declared in 1698 that "one can neither, in surety of conscience,
buy nor sell Negroes, because in such commerce there is injustice." In any case, as an
eighteenth-century prelate, Cardinal Gerdil, categorically stated, "Slavery is not to be
understood as conferring on one man the same power over another that men have over
cattle. . . . For slavery does not abolish the natural equality of man. . . ."

At the same time the church, in its character as an institution, functioning in the
society of men, could not afford to proscribe slavery as unconditionally immoral, if for
no other reason than that the majority of Christendom's overseas dominions would thus

* Haring, *Spanish Empire*, p. 219. It has to be added that one year after Charles's retirement to the monastery
of Saint-Just in 1558, slavery and the slave trade was resumed.

have been stained in depravity—a position which, for almost any procedural purposes, would have been absurdly untenable. Its casuists, therefore, readily found sanctions in tradition whereby slavery might exist under the church's official favor. Thus the Council of the Indies, after meetings with theologians, jurists, and prelates of the church, assured the king of Spain that

> . . . *there cannot be any doubt as to the necessity of those slaves for the support of the kingdom of the Indies . . . ; and [that] with regard to the point of conscience, [the trade may continue] because of the reasons expressed, the authorities cited, and its longlived and general custom in the kingdoms of Castile, America, and Portugal, without any objection on the part of his Holiness or ecclesiastical state, but rather with the tolerance of all of them.*

The Jesuits would labor excessively in places such as Brazil to mitigate the evils of slavery; the papacy itself would denounce it in various ways in 1462, 1537, 1639, 1741, 1815, and 1839; at the same time the church "could no more have proclaimed the abolition of slavery," as Fr. Rinchon remarks, "than it could have imposed the eight-hour day or the rate of family incomes."

Yet in the very act of certifying the practice of slavery, in admitting its economic necessity, and even in holding slaves of its own, the church had, as it were, bargained with the system so that its own institutional needs and its prerogatives in matters of morality might still be maintained at the visible maximum and protected against infringement. The effects of this determination are overwhelmingly evident in the actual workings of slavery in Latin America. They are evident, indeed, at nearly every point in the traffic itself, for the potent hand of the church fell upon the sequence of events long before it terminated in America. It had missionaries on the soil of Africa, proselytizing among the natives and operating great establishments there. It was highly sensitive to the possibility that the Faith, in the course of the trade, might be corrupted. In 1685 the Inquisition, faced with an impending transaction which would turn over a portion of the trade to the Dutch, sternly urged the king that,

> . . . *in case any contract is made with the Dutch, you will please to ordain that all necessary orders be provided and issued for the utmost care of the conservation and purity of our Holy Catholic Faith, because one can very justly fear that if the negroes come by way of the Dutch, they may be greatly imbued with doctrines and errors . . . and . . . this council should advise the inquisitors to exercise special vigilance.*

The contract was eventually made, but the Dutchman who received it was forced to take ten Capuchin monks to his African factories for the religious instruction of the Negroes, to support them, and to allow them to preach in public. The Inquisition had a tribunal in the Indies which would punish any "heretic" (meaning Dutch or Flemish) who tried to introduce his creed there during the course of business. Every slave bound for Brazil was to receive baptism and religious instruction before being put on board, and upon reaching port every ship was boarded by a friar who examined the conscience, faith, and religion of the new arrivals. The friar was there "to investigate the individual's orthodoxy just as today the immigrant's health and race are investigated."

It would be misleading to imply that slavery in the colonies drew its total character from the powerful influence of the church. But it may be asserted that the church, functioning in its capacity as guardian of morals, was responsible for whatever human rights were conserved for the slave within the grim system. What it came to was that three formidable interests—the crown, the planter, and the church—were deeply concerned with the system, that these concerns were in certain ways competing, and that the product of this balance of power left its profound impress on the actual legal and customary sanctions governing the status and treatment of slaves. These sanctions were by no means what they would have been had it been left to the planting class alone to develop them systematically with reference only to the requirements of a labor system. Let us examine them, taking the same rough categories used with respect to the American South: term of servitude, marriage and the family, police and discipline, and property and other civil rights.

Neither in Brazil nor in Spanish America did slavery carry with it such precise and irrevocable categories of perpetual servitude, *"durante vita"* and "for all generations," as in the United States. The presumption in these countries, should the status of a colored person be in doubt, was that he was free rather than a slave. There were in fact innumerable ways whereby a slave's servitude could be brought to an end. The chief of these was the very considerable fact that he might buy his own freedom. The Negro in Cuba or Mexico had the right to have his price declared and could, if he wished, purchase himself in installments. Slaves escaping to Cuba to embrace Catholicism were protected by a special royal order of 1733 which was twice reissued. A slave unduly punished might be set at liberty by the magistrate. In Brazil the slave who was the parent of ten children might legally demand his or her freedom. The medieval Spanish code had made a slave's service terminable under any number of contingencies—if he denounced cases of treason, murder, counterfeiting, or the rape of a virgin, or if he performed various other kinds of meritorious acts. Though all such practices did not find their way into the seventeenth- and eighteenth-century legal arrangements of Latin America, much of their spirit was perpetuated in the values, customs, and social expectations of that later period. It is important to appreciate the high social approval connected with the freeing of slaves. A great variety of happy family events—the birth of a son, the marriage of a daughter, anniversaries, national holidays—provided the occasion, and their ceremonial was frequently marked by the manumission of one or more virtuous servitors. It was considered a pious act to accept the responsibility of becoming godfather to a slave child, implying the moral obligation to arrange eventually for its freedom. Indeed, in Cuba and Brazil such freedom might be purchased for a nominal sum at the baptismal font. All such manumissions had the strong approval of both church and state and were registered gratis by the government.

In extending its moral authority over men of every condition, the church naturally insisted on bringing slave unions under the holy sacraments. Slaves were married in church and the banns published; marriage was a sacred rite and its sanctity protected in law. In the otherwise circumspect United States, the only category which the law could apply to conjugal relations between slaves—or to unions between master and slave—was concubinage. But concubinage, in Latin America, was condemned as licentious, adulterous, and immoral; safeguards against promiscuity were provided in the law, and in Brazil the Jesuits labored mightily to regularize the libertinage of the master class by the sacrament of Christian marriage. Moreover, slaves owned by different masters were not to be hindered from marrying, nor could they be kept separate after marriage. If the estates were distant, the wife was to go with her husband, and a fair price was to be fixed by impartial persons for her sale to the husband's master. A slave might, without legal interference, marry a free person. The children of such a marriage, if the mother were free, were themselves free, inasmuch as children followed the condition of their mother.

The master's disciplinary authority never had the completeness that it had in the United States, and nowhere did he enjoy powers of life and death over the slave's body. Under the Spanish code of 1789 slaves might be punished for failure to perform their duties, with prison, chains, or lashes, "which last must not exceed the number of twenty-five, and those must be given them in such manner as not to cause any contusion or effusion of blood: which punishments cannot be imposed on slaves but by their masters or the stewards." For actual crimes a slave was to be tried in an ordinary court of justice like any free person, and, conversely, the murder of a slave was to be prosecuted just as that of a free man would be. Excessive punishments of slaves—causing "contusion, effusion of blood, or mutilation of members"—by plantation stewards were themselves punishable. Although gross violations of the law occurred, the law here was anything but the dead letter it proved to be in our own southern states. In the important administrative centers of both Brazil and the Spanish colonies there was an official protector of slaves, known variously as the syndic, procurador, or attorney-general, under whose jurisdiction came all matters relating to the treatment of slaves. His functions were nurtured by a well-articulated system of communications. The priests who made the regular rounds of the estates giving Christian instruction were required to obtain and render to him information from the slaves regarding their treatment, and investigation and the necessary steps would be taken accordingly. These priests were answerable to no one else for their activities. In addition, the magistrates were to appoint "persons of good character" to visit the estates thrice yearly and conduct similar inquiries on similar matters. A further ingenious provision in the Spanish code caused all fines levied, for mistreatment and other excesses against slaves, to be divided up three ways: one-third went to the judge, one-third to the informer, and one-third to the "Fines Chest." Finally, the attorney-general and the justices themselves were made accountable to the crown for failure to carry out these ordinances. An implicit royal threat underlay all this; should the fines not have the desired effect and should the ordinances continue to be broken, "I," His Majesty promised, "will take my measures accordingly."

As was implied in his right to purchase his own freedom, the slave in the Spanish and Portuguese colonies had the right to acquire and hold property. This meant something specific; in Brazil a master was obliged by law to give liberty to his slaves on all Sundays and holidays—which totaled eighty-five in the year—during which a slave might work for himself and accumulate money for his purchase price, and the Spanish code of 1789 provided that slaves must be allowed two hours each day in which to be employed in "occupations for their own advantage." In many places slaves were encouraged to hire themselves out regularly (there were skilled artisans among them as

well as ordinary laborers), an arrangement which was to the advantage of both the
master and the slave himself, since the latter was allowed to keep a percentage of the
wage. Slaves even in rural areas might sell the produce of their gardens and retain the
proceeds. For all practical purposes slavery here had become, as Mr. Tannenbaum puts
it, a contractual arrangement: it could be wiped out by a fixed purchase price and leave
no taint. "There may have been no written contract between the two parties, but the
state behaved, in effect, as if such a contract did exist, and used its powers to enforce it."
It was a contract in which the master owned a man's labor but not the man.

As for the privileges of religion, it was here not a question of the planting class
"permitting" the slave, under rigidly specified conditions, to take part in divine
worship. It was rather a matter of the church's insisting—under its own
conditions—that masters bring their slaves to church and teach them religion. Such a
man as the Mississippi planter who directed that the gospel preached to his slaves
should be "in its original purity and simplicity" would have courted the full wrath of
the Latin church. A Caribbean synod of 1622, whose *sanctiones* had the force of law,
made lengthy provisions for the chastisement of masters who prevented their slaves
from hearing Mass or receiving instruction on feast days. Here the power of the Faith
was such that master and slave stood equally humbled before it. "Every one who has
slaves," according to the first item in the Spanish code, "is obliged to instruct them in
the principles of the Roman Catholic religion and in the necessary truths in order that
the slaves may be baptized within the (first) year of their residence in the Spanish
dominions." Certain assumptions were implied therein which made it impossible that
the slave in this culture should ever quite be considered as mere property, either in law
or in society's customary habits of mind. These assumptions, perpetuated and fostered
by the church, made all the difference in his treatment by society and its institutions,
not only while a slave, but also if and when he should cease to be one. They were, in
effect, that he was a man, that he had a soul as precious as any other man's, that he had
a moral nature, that he was not only as susceptible to sin but also as eligible for grace as
his master—that master and slave were brothers in Christ.

The Spaniards and Portuguese had the widespread reputation by the eighteenth
century—whatever may have been the reasons—for being among all nations the best
masters of slaves. The standards for such a judgment cannot, of course, be made too
simple. Were slaves "physically maltreated" in those countries? They could,
conceivably, have been treated worse than in our own nineteenth-century South without
altering the comparison, for even in cruelty the relationship was between man and man.
Was there "race prejudice"? No one could be more arrogantly proud of his racial purity
than the Spaniard of Castile, and theoretically there were rigid caste lines, but the finest
Creole families, the clergy, the army, the professions, were hopelessly "defiled" by
Negro blood; the taboos were that vague in practice. Was there squalor, filth,
widespread depression of the masses? Much more so than with us—but there it was the
class system and economic "underdevelopment," rather than the color barrier, that made
the difference. In these countries the concept of "beyond the pale" applied primarily to
beings outside the Christian fold rather than to those beyond the color line.

We are not, then, dealing with a society steeped, like our own, in traditions of
political and economic democracy. We are concerned only with a special and peculiar

kind of fluidity—that of their slave systems—and in this alone lay a world of difference. It was a fluidity that permitted a transition from slavery to freedom that was smooth, organic, and continuing. Manumitting slaves, carrying as it did such high social approval, was done often, and the spectacle of large numbers of freedmen was familiar to the social scene. Such opportunities as were open to any member of the depressed classes who had talent and diligence were open as well to the ex-slave and his descendants. Thus color itself was no grave disability against taking one's place in free society; indeed, Anglo-Saxon travelers in nineteenth-century Brazil were amazed at the thoroughgoing mixture of races there. "I have passed black ladies in silks and jewelry," wrote Thomas Ewbank in the 1850's, "with male slaves in livery behind them. . . . Several have white husbands. The first doctor of the city is a colored man; so is the President of the Province." Free Negroes had the same rights before the law as whites, and it was possible for the most energetic of their numbers to take immediate part in public and professional life. Among the Negroes and mulattoes of Brazil and the Spanish colonies—aside from the swarming numbers of skilled craftsmen—were soldiers, officers, musicians, poets, priests, and judges. "I am accustomed," said a delegate to the Cortes of Cádiz in 1811, "to seeing many engaged in all manner of careers."

All such rights and opportunities existed *before* the abolition of slavery; and thus we may note it as no paradox that emancipation, when it finally did take place, was brought about in all these Latin-American countries "without violence, without bloodshed, and without civil war."

fifteen
comparative cruelty
and violence
in latin america and
the united states

DAVID BRION DAVIS

*David Brion Davis (b. 1927) is professor of history at Yale University,
taught at Cornell University, and has served as Harmsworth Professor
of American History at Oxford University. In 1967 he was awarded
the Pulitzer Prize for his book* The Problem of Slavery in Western
Culture *(1966), which examined the concept and institution of slavery
in European history and the Western hemisphere. Among his other
publications are* Homicide in American Fiction, 1798–1860 *(1968)
and* The Slave Power Conspiracy and the Paranoid Style *(1970).
In studying this selection and comparing it with Elkins's the reader is
faced with the basic question: How does one evaluate these two
interpretations of slavery in Latin America and the United States?*

By the late eighteenth century most travelers agreed that in
Brazil and the Spanish colonies the condition of slaves was
considerably better than in British America. Any comparison
must consider Negro slavery as a system of forced labor, of social
organization, and of class and racial discipline. Numerous
accounts from the late eighteenth and nineteenth centuries tell us
that the Latin American slave enjoyed frequent hours of leisure

Source: David Brion Davis, *The Problem of Slavery in Western Culture* (Ithaca,
N.Y.: Cornell University Press, 1966), pp. 227–38, 242–43. Footnotes omitted.
Copyright © 1966 by Cornell University. Used by permission of Cornell
University Press.

and was seldom subjected to the factory-like regimentation that characterized the
capitalistic plantations of the north; that he faced no legal bars to marriage, education,
or eventual freedom; that he was legally protected from cruelty and oppression, and was
not stigmatized on account of his race. This relative felicity has quite plausibly been
attributed to a culture that de-emphasized the pursuit of private profit, to the Catholic
Church's insistence on the slave's right to marry and worship, and to what Gilberto
Freyre has termed the "miscibility" of the Portuguese, which submerged sensitivity to
racial difference in a frank acceptance of sexual desire.

No doubt there is much truth in even the idyllic picture of the Brazilian "Big
House," where slaves and freemen pray and loaf together, and where masters shrug
their shoulders at account books and prefer to frolic with slave girls in shaded
hammocks. But we should not forget that West Indian and North American planters
were fond of idealizing their own "Big Houses" as patriarchal manors, of portraying
their Negroes as carefree and indolent, and of proudly displaying humane slave laws
which they knew to be unenforceable. Their propaganda, which was supported by
travelers' accounts and which long seemed persuasive to many Northerners and
Englishmen, has largely been discredited by numerous critical studies based on a wealth
of surviving evidence. Many of the records of Brazilian slavery were destroyed in the
1890's, in a fit of abolitionist enthusiasm, and the subject has never received the careful
scrutiny it deserves. Only in recent years have such historians as Octávio Ianni,
Fernando Henrique Cardoso, Jaime Jaramillo Uribe, and C. R. Boxer begun to
challenge the stereotyped images of mild servitude and racial harmony.

There is little reason to doubt that slavery in Latin America, compared with that in
North America, was less subject to the pressures of competitive capitalism and was
closer to a system of patriarchal rights and semifeudalistic services. But after granting
this, we must recognize the inadequacy of thinking in terms of idealized models of
patriarchal and capitalistic societies. Presumably, an exploitive, capitalistic form of
servitude could not exist within a patriarchal society. The lord of a manor, unlike the
entrepreneur who might play the role of lord of a manor, would be incapable of treating
men as mere units of labor in a speculative enterprise. But neither would he think of
exploring new lands, discovering gold mines, or developing new plantations for the
production of sugar and coffee. It is perhaps significant that accounts of Latin American
slavery often picture the relaxed life on sugar plantations after their decline in economic
importance, and ignore conditions that prevailed during the Brazilian sugar boom of the
seventeenth century, the mining boom of the early eighteenth century, and the coffee
boom of the nineteenth century. Similarly, Southern apologists tended to overlook the
human effects of high-pressure agriculture in the Southwest, and focus their attention
on the easygoing and semipatriarchal societies of tidewater Maryland and Virginia.
Eugene D. Genovese has recently suggested that while the North American slave
system was stimulated and exploited by the capitalist world market, it retained many
precapitalistic features, such as a lack of innovation, restricted markets, and low
productivity of labor, and actually gravitated toward an uneconomical paternalism that
was basically antithetical to capitalistic values.

Although a particular instance of oppression or well-being can always be dismissed as
an exception, it is important to know what range of variation a system permitted. If an

exploitive, capitalistic form of servitude was at times common in Brazil and Spanish America, and if North Americans conformed at times to a paternalistic model and openly acknowledged the humanity of their slaves, it may be that differences between slavery in Latin America and the United States were no greater than regional or temporal differences within the countries themselves. And such a conclusion would lead us to suspect that Negro bondage was a single phenomenon, or *Gestalt*, whose variations were less significant than underlying patterns of unity.

Simon Gray, a Natchez river boatman, provides us with an example of the flexibility of the North American slave system. During the 1850's, most Southern states tightened their laws and to all appearances erected an impassable barrier between the worlds of slave and freeman. But the intent of legislators was often offset by powerful forces of economic interest and personality. Simon Gray was an intelligent slave whose superior abilities were recognized by both his master and the lumber company which hired his services. In the 1850's this lowly slave became the captain of a flatboat on the Mississippi, supervising and paying wages to a crew that included white men. In defiance of law, Gray was permitted to carry firearms, to travel freely on his own, to build and run sawmills, and to conduct commercial transactions as his company's agent. Entrusted with large sums of money for business purposes, Gray also drew a regular salary, rented a house where his family lived in privacy, and took a vacation to Hot Springs, Arkansas, when his health declined. Although there is evidence that in Southern industry and commerce such privileges were not as uncommon as has been assumed, we may be sure that Simon Gray was a very exceptional slave. He might well have been less exceptional in Cuba or Brazil. The essential point, however, is that regardless of restrictive laws, the Southern slave system had room for a few Simon Grays. The flatboat captain could not have acted as he did if the society had demanded a rigorous enforcement of the law.

By the time Simon Gray was beginning to enjoy relative freedom, Portugal and Brazil were the only civilized nations that openly resisted attempts to suppress the African slave trade. It has been estimated that by 1853 Britain had paid Portugal some £2,850,965 in bribes intended to stop a commerce whose horrors had multiplied as a result of efforts to escape detection and capture. But despite British bribes and seizures, the trade continued, and was countenanced by the society which has been most praised for its humane treatment of slaves. One of the boats captured by the British, in 1842, was a tiny vessel of eighteen tons, whose crew consisted of six Portuguese. Between decks, in a space only eighteen inches high, they had intended to stow two hundred and fifty African children of about seven years of age. Suspicion of Britain's motives probably prevented more outspoken attacks on a trade that outraged most of the civilized world. But the fact remains that Brazilian society not only permitted the slave trade to continue for nearly half a century after it had been outlawed by Britain and the United States, but provided a flourishing market for Negroes fresh from Africa. During the 1830's Brazil imported more than 400,000 slaves; in the single year of 1848 the nation absorbed some sixty thousand more. That the reception of these newcomers was not so humane as might be imagined is suggested by a law of 1869, six years after Lincoln's Emancipation Proclamation, which forbade the separate sale of husband and wife, or of children under fifteen. Not long before, even children under ten had been separated from their parents and sent to the coffee plantations of the south.

These examples are intended only to illustrate the range of variation that could occur in any slave society, and hence the difficulties in comparing the relative severity of slave systems. Barbados and Jamaica were notorious for their harsh laws and regimentation, but occasional proprietors like Josiah Steele or Matthew Lewis succeeded in creating model plantations where Negroes were accorded most of the privileges of white servants. John Stedman, who provided Europe with ghastly pictures of the cruelty of Dutch masters in Surinam, also maintained that humanity and gentleness coexisted with the worst barbarity. The well-being of any group of slaves was subject to many variables. It seems certain that the few Negroes in eighteenth-century Québec lived a freer and richer life than hundreds of thousands of slaves in nineteenth-century Brazil and Cuba, despite the fact that the latter were technically guarded by certain legal protections, and the former were defined as chattels completely subject to their owners' authority. Islands like Dominica and Saint Lucia, which were disorganized by war and a transfer from one nation to another, had few social resources for restraining the unscrupulous master or curbing slave resistance. In the newly developed lands of captured or ceded colonies, such as Berbice, Demerara, Trinidad, and Louisiana, there were few effective checks on the speculative planter bent on reaping maximum profit in the shortest possible time. And whereas the North American slave frequently lived in a land of peace and plentiful food, his West Indian brother was the first to feel the pinch of famine when war cut off essential supplies, or when his master was burdened by debt and declining profits. On the small tobacco farms of colonial Virginia and Maryland the physical condition of slaves was surely better than in the mines of Minas Gerais or on the great plantations of Bahia, where a Capuchin missionary was told in 1682 that a Negro who endured for seven years was considered to have lived very long.

North American planters were fond of comparing the fertility of their own slaves with the high mortality and low birth rate of those in the West Indies and Latin America, and of concluding that theirs was the milder and more humane system. Such reasoning failed to take account of the low proportion of female slaves in the West Indies, the communicable diseases transmitted by the African trade, and the high incidence of tetanus and other maladies that were particularly lethal to infants in the Caribbean. No doubt differences in sanitation and nutrition, rather than in physical treatment, explain the fact that while Brazil and the United States each entered the nineteenth century with about a million slaves, and subsequent importations into Brazil were three times greater than those into the United States, by the Civil War there were nearly four million slaves in the United States and only one and one-half million in Brazil. But after all such allowances are made, it still seems probable that planters in Brazil and the West Indies, who were totally dependent on fresh supplies of labor from Africa, were less sensitive than North Americans to the value of human life. When a slave's life expectancy was a few years at most, and when each slave could easily be replaced, there was little incentive to improve conditions or limit hours of work. According to both C. R. Boxer and Celso Furtado, Brazilian sugar planters took a short-term view of their labor needs, and accepted the axiom, which spread to the

British Caribbean, that it was good economy to work one's slaves to death and then purchase more. In colonial Brazil, Jesuit priests felt it necessary to admonish overseers not to kick pregnant women in the stomach or beat them with clubs, since this brought a considerable loss in slave property.

But what of the benevolent laws of Latin America which allowed a slave to marry, to seek relief from a cruel master, and even to purchase his own freedom? It must be confessed that on this crucial subject historians have been overly quick to believe what travelers passed on from conversations with slaveholders, and to make glowing generalizations on the basis of one-sided evidence.

Much has been made of the fact that the Spanish model law, *las Siete Partidas*, recognized freedom as man's natural state, and granted the slave certain legal protections. But the argument loses some of its point when we learn that the same principles were accepted in North American law, and that *las Siete Partidas* not only made the person and possessions of the bondsman totally subject to his master's will, but even gave owners the right to kill their slaves in certain circumstances. Some of the early Spanish and Portuguese legislation protecting Indians has erroneously been thought to have extended to Negroes as well. In actuality, the first laws pertaining to Negroes in such colonies as Chile, Panama, and New Granada were designed to prohibit them from carrying arms, from moving about at night, and above all, from fraternizing with Indians. It is true that in the late seventeenth and early eighteenth centuries the Portuguese crown issued edicts intended to prevent the gross mistreatment of Negro slaves. But as C. R. Boxer has pointed out, Brazilian law was a chaotic tangle of Manueline and Filipine codes, encrusted by numerous decrees which often contradicted one another, and which were interpreted by lawyers and magistrates notorious for their dishonesty. Even if this had not been true, slaves were dispersed over immense areas where there were few towns and where justice was administered by local magnates whose power lay in land and slaves. It is not surprising that in one of the few recorded cases of the Portuguese crown intervening to investigate the torture of a slave, nothing was done to the accused owner. This revisionist view receives support from Jaime Jaramillo Uribe's conclusion that the judicial system of New Granada was so ineffective that even the reform legislation of the late eighteenth century did little to change the oppressive life of Negro slaves.

In theory, of course, the Portuguese or Spanish slave possessed an immortal soul that entitled him to respect as a human personality. But though perfunctorily baptized in Angola or on the Guinea coast, he was appraised and sold like any merchandise upon his arrival in America. Often slaves were herded in mass, stark naked, into large warehouses where they were examined and marketed like animals. As late as the mid-nineteenth century the spread of disease among newly arrived Negroes who were crowded into the warehouses of Rio de Janeiro brought widespread fears of epidemic. The Spanish, who ordinarily sold horses and cows individually, purchased Negroes in lots, or *piezas de Indias*, which were sorted according to age and size. There is abundant evidence that Brazilians were little troubled by the separation of Negro families; in the 1850's coffee planters in the rich Parahyba Valley thought nothing of selling their own illegitimate children to passing traders. Despite protests from priests and governors, it was also common practice for Brazilians to purchase attractive girls who could profitably be let out as prostitutes.

In Brazil, as in other slave societies, there were apparently authentic reports of bondsmen being boiled alive, roasted in furnaces, or subjected to other fiendish punishments. More significant than such extreme cases of sadism is the evidence that planters who were successful and were accepted as social leaders equipped their estates with the chambers and instruments of torture; that it was common custom to punish a recalcitrant slave with *novenas*, which meant that he would be tied down and flogged for nine to thirteen consecutive nights, his cuts sometimes being teased with a razor and rubbed with salt and urine. In the mid-eighteenth century, Manuel Ribeiro Rocha attacked the Brazilian "rural theology" which allowed masters to welcome their new slaves with a vicious whipping, to work them in the fields without rest, and to inflict one hundred or more lashes without cause. A century later planters in the Parahyba Valley taught their sons that Negroes were not true men but inferior beings who could only be controlled by continued punishment; and some of the clergy maintained that Africans were the condemned sons of Cain. This widespread conviction of racial inferiority justified a regime of hatred and brutality in which the slave had no right of appeal and even fatal beatings went unpunished.

Obviously much depended on regional differences in economy and social tradition. The recent studies of the extreme southern provinces of Brazil by Octávio Ianni and Fernando Cardoso reveal a picture of harsh chattel slavery and racial prejudice which stands in marked contrast to the familiar images of benign servitude in the north. During the last third of the eighteenth century the southern states developed a capitalistic economy which was initially stimulated by the export of wheat but which came to rely heavily on the production of jerked beef.* Whether engaged in agriculture, stock raising, or the processing of meat or leather, the slaveholding capitalists were bent on maximizing production for commercial profit. Because the economy rested on slave labor and physical labor was largely associated with the African race, Negroes and mulattoes were regarded as mere instruments of production, wholly lacking in human personality. According to Ianni, the slave was a totally alienated being; able to express himself only through the intermediary of his owner, he was under the complete dominion of a master class which rigidly controlled his movements and held power over his life and death. Though kind and paternalistic masters were to be found in Paraná, Santa Catarina, and Rio Grande do Sul, as elsewhere in the Americas, the overriding fact is that the ideology and judicial framework of southern Brazil were geared to the maintenance of an exploitive system of labor, to the preservation of public security, and to the perpetuation of power in the hands of a white ruling caste. At every point the Negro was forced to shape his behavior in accordance with the actions and expectations of the white man.

Conditions were undoubtedly better in the cities, where protective laws were more often enforced and where Negroes had at least a chance of acquiring money that could purchase freedom. But in colonial Cartagena, Negro slaves were subject to the most repressive police regulations, and to punishments which ranged from death to the

---

* The term "southern states" refers to the southern provinces of Brazil.

cutting off of hands, ears, or the penis. In Mariana the city councilors demanded in 1755 that the right to purchase freedom be withdrawn and that slaves who tried to escape be crippled for life. While both proposals aroused the indignation of the viceroy at Bahia, they indicate the state of mind of a master class which, in Minas Gerais, posted the heads of fugitive slaves along the roadsides. And men who accepted such brutality as a necessary part of life could not always be expected to abandon their fields or shut down their sugar mills on thirty-five religious holidays, in addition to fifty-two Sundays. It was not an idyllic, semifeudal servitude that made colonial Brazil widely known as "the hell for Negroes," and as a place where their lives would be "nasty, brutish, and short"; or that drove countless bondsmen to suicide or revolt, and reduced others to a state of psychic shock, of flat apathy and depression, which was common enough in Brazil to acquire the special name of *banzo.* . . .

In conclusion, it would appear that the image of the warmly human Big House must be balanced by a counterimage of the brutal society of the coffee barons, who even in the 1870's and 1880's governed a world in which there were no gradations between slavery and freedom. In their deep-rooted racial prejudice, their military-like discipline, their bitter resistance to any restrictions on a slaveowner's will, their constant fear of insurrection and their hostility toward meaningful religious instruction of their Negroes, these planters were hardly superior to their brothers in Mississippi. Even with the approach of inevitable emancipation, they made no effort to prepare their slaves for freedom. It was in the face of this "slave power" that the Brazilian abolitionists resorted to the familiar demands for "immediate" and "unconditional" emancipation, and modeled themselves on the champions of British and American reform. Joaquim Nabuco, the great leader of the Brazilian antislavery movement, adopted the pen name of "Garrison."

With the exception of legal barriers to manumission . . . , the salient traits of North American slavery were to be found among the Spanish and Portuguese. Notwithstanding variations within every colony as a result of environment, economic conditions, social institutions, and the personality of owners, the Negro was everywhere a mobile and transferable possession whose labor and well-being were controlled by another man. Any comparison of slavery in North and South America should take account of the fact that Brazil alone had an area and variety comparable to all British America, and that the privileged artisans, porters, and domestic servants of colonial Brazilian cities can be compared only with their counterparts in New York and Philadelphia. Similarly, conditions in nineteenth-century Alabama and Mississippi must be held against those in the interior coffee-growing areas of south-central Brazil. Given the lack of detailed statistical information, we can only conclude that the subject is too complex and the evidence too contradictory for us to assume that the treatment of slaves was substantially better in Latin America than in the British colonies, taken as a whole.

selected
bibliography

PRIMARY SOURCES

Scholarly monographs and articles are essential to the study of
Afro-American slavery, but they can never replace the
atmosphere nor provide the insight into the "peculiar
institution" that can be gathered from research in the primary
sources. An examination of autobiographies written by ex-slaves
illustrates slave life, interpersonal relationships, and
psychological development. Considered to be most revealing and
free of abolitionist tampering are: Frederick Douglass, the most
famous black abolitionist, *Narrative of the Life of Frederick
Douglass* (Boston: 1845) and *My Bondage and My Freedom* (New
York: 1855); William Wells Brown, a noted black abolitionist,
Narrative of William Wells Brown (Boston: 1847); Solomon
Northupt, the revelations of a Northern free Negro kidnapped
and sold into slavery, *Twelve Years a Slave* (Auburn, N.Y.: 1853);
Lunsford Lane, autobiography of a North Carolina ex-slave who
purchased his wife's freedom, *The Narrative of Lunsford Lane*
(Boston: 1842); James Pennington, who became an influential
black clergyman, *The Fugitive Blacksmith* (London: 1849).
Olaudah Equiano's autobiography, *The Interesting Life of Olaudah
Equiano, or Gustavus Vassa, the African* (London: 1789), is
particularly valuable for its description of his capture, sale into
slavery, and the middle passage.

Three unpublished doctoral dissertations provide information
on the origins of many slave narratives and demonstrate the
utility of valid autobiographies to an analysis of slavery: Marion
W. Starling, "The Slave Narrative: Its Place in American
Literary History" (New York University, 1946); Charles H.
Nichols, Jr., "A Study of the Slave Narrative" (Brown
University, 1948); Margaret Young Jackson, "An Investigation
of Biographies and Autobiographies of American Slaves
Published between 1840 and 1860: Based upon the Cornell
Special Slavery Collection" (Cornell University, 1954).

Interviews with ex-slaves are another useful primary source
describing slave life and attitudes; however, most of the

recollections were collected long after slavery had ended when the ex-slaves were quite old. The most extensive of the interview studies was that undertaken by the Federal Writers Project during the 1930s of ex-slaves, descendants of ex-slaves, and white informants. The original typescripts of over two thousand narratives and several hundred photographs have been collated, arranged in seventeen volumes in thirty-three parts (now available in microfilm copy), and deposited in the Rare Books Division of the Library of Congress. A sampling of these narratives has been published in *Lay My Burden Down: A Folk History of Slavery* (Chicago: 1945) edited by B. A. Botkin. Other studies employing traditional sources as well as ex-slave interviews were prepared by the Virginia and Louisiana Work Projects Administrations: *The Negro in Virginia* (New York: 1940) and *Drums and Shadows: Survival Studies among the Georgia Coastal Negroes* (Athens, Ga.: 1940). The Fisk University study, *Unwritten History of Slavery* (Mimeograph, Nashville: 1945), also employs this oral history technique. Letters written by slaves and free blacks are also valuable tools, particularly the collections of Carter G. Woodson, ed., *The Mind of the Negro as Reflected in Letters Written During the Crisis* (Washington, D.C.: 1926). Herbert Aptheker's *Documentary History of the Negro People in the United States*, Vol. I (New York: 1951) is a superb collection of primary sources through the Civil War.

Accounts by nineteenth-century travelers and female residents are also valuable sources of information. The best ones include Charles Lyell, *Travels in North America* (London: 1845); Frederick Law Olmstead, *A Journey in the Seaboard Slave States* (New York: 1856) and *The Cotton Kingdom* (New York: 1861); Harriet Martineau, *Society in America* (New York: 1837); Frances Ann Kemble, *Journal of a Residence on a Georgia Plantation in 1838–1839* (New York: 1863); William H. Russell, *My Diary North and South* (Boston: 1863); Alexis de Tocqueville, *Democracy in America* (Paris: 1850).

SECONDARY SOURCES

BIBLIOGRAPHIC AIDS

The most comprehensive bibliographies on slavery and Afro-American history are: William L. Katz, *Teachers' Guide to American Negro History*, rev. ed. (New York: 1971); Elizabeth W. Miller, *The Negro in America: A Bibliography* (Cambridge: 1966); and Erwin K. Welsch, *The Negro in the United States, A Research Guide* (Bloomington, Ind.: 1966). John Hope Franklin's *From Slavery to Freedom* (New York: 1967) is the most comprehensive history of Afro-Americans with an excellent bibliography.

AFRICA AND THE SLAVE TRADE

There are, of course, particular aspects of the history of slavery not covered in this reader. An understanding of the African influence in Afro-American culture, the slave reaction to bondage, and personality development necessitates a familiarity with African history and culture. The best general studies of African civilization are: Carter G. Woodson, *African Background Outlined* (Washington, D.C.: 1936). Woodson, a black historian with a Ph.D. from Harvard, was a pioneer in the Negro history movement; Melville Herskovits, *The Myth of the Negro Past* (New York: 1941) Herskovits was an anthropologist and a pioneer in the study of blacks in Africa and the New World; Roland Oliver and J. D. Fage are two leading English Africanists who wrote *A Short History of Africa* (2d ed., Baltimore: 1966); Robert July, an American Africanist, wrote *A History of the African People* (New York: 1970); E. W. Bovill's *The Golden Trade of the Moors* (2d ed., London: 1968) is particularly valuable for its study of the trans-Sahara trade between North Africa and the ancient kingdoms of West Africa. Since most Afro-Americans are descendants of West Africa, several studies of West African history deserve consideration: Basil Davidson, *A History of West Africa* (London: 1965); A. A. Boahen, *Topics in West African History* (London: 1966); J. F. Ade Ajayi and Ian Espie, eds., *A Thousand Years of West African History* (London: 1965).

The slave trade has often raised vigorous debate concerning the numbers brought to the New World, mortality rates as a result of the slave trade, the utilitarian or humanitarian reasons for its suppression, and the mechanics of its suppression. Four general histories of the slave trade are: Basil Davidson, *The African Slave Trade* (Boston: 1961); Daniel Mannix and Malcolm Cowley, *Black Cargoes* (New York: 1962); John Pope-Hennessey, *Sins of the Fathers: A Study of the Atlantic Slave Traders* (New York: 1968); H. A. Wyndham, *The Atlantic and Slavery* (London 1935). Philip Curtin's *The Atlantic Slave Trade: A Census* (Madison, Wis.: 1969) is the most recent analysis of the numerical extent of the slave trade. Primary sources relevant to the slave trade have been collected by Elizabeth Donnan, ed., in her very valuable *Documents Illustrative of the Slave Trade to America*, 4 vols. (Washington, D.C.: 1930–1935).

Several studies have been concerned with the movement to abolish the slave trade. Reginald Coupland's *The British Antislavery Movement* (London: 1933) emphasizes the humanitarian motivation of the antislave trade movement. The politics involved in ending the American slave trade is covered by W. E. B. DuBois, *The Suppression of the African Slave Trade* (Cambridge, Mass.: 1896). DuBois was the first black to receive the Ph.D. from Harvard University; his study was the first volume of the Harvard Historical Studies which were the first series of scholarly works to be published by an American university. More recent studies are: Peter Duigan and C. Clendenen, *The United States and the African Slave Trade, 1619–1862* (Stanford, Calif.: 1963) and Howard S. Warren, *American Slavers and the Federal Law, 1837–1862* (Berkeley, Calif.: 1963).

THE ORIGINS OF SLAVERY IN COLONIAL AMERICA

The most complete account of the beginning of slavery in the colonies is Winthrop D. Jordan's prizewinning *White over Black: American Attitudes toward the Negro, 1550–1812* (Chapel Hill, N.C.: 1968). It may be supplemented with Paul C. Palmer, "Servant into Slave: The Evolution of the Legal Status of the Negro in Colonial Virginia," *South Atlantic Quarterly* 65 (1966); Eugene Sirmans, "The Legal Status of the Slave in South Carolina, 1670–1740," *Journal of Southern History* 28 (November 1962). Other worthwhile studies of slavery in the colonial period on the state and local levels, although not dealing specifically with the origins of slavery, are: Thad W. Tate, *The Negro in Eighteenth Century Williamsburg* (Williamsburg: 1965); Lorenzo J. Greene, *The*

Negro in Colonial New England (New York: 1942); Peter H. Wood, *Black Majority: Negroes in Colonial South Carolina* (New York: 1974).

The American Revolution gave impetus to the Northern abolition movement, provided a role for blacks as soldiers, and increased the anxiety of the early republic over the presence of slaves in America. The antislavery impact of the Revolution is considered in Arthur Zilversmit's incisive study of emancipation in the Northern states, *The First Emancipation* (Chicago: 1967). The role of the black soldier in the War for Independence is discussed in George H. Moore, *Historical Notes on the Employment of Negroes in the American Army of the Revolution* (New York: 1862) and the excellent study of Benjamin Quarles, *The Negro in the American Revolution* (Chapel Hill, N.C.: 1961). The following studies consider the views of America's founding fathers on the question of continued slavery: Thomas Jefferson's *Notes on the State of Virginia* (London: 1787) reveals his doubts that a white and a freed black population could live in tranquillity in America; William Cohen, "Thomas Jefferson and the Problem of Slavery," *American Historical Review* 61 (December 1969); William W. Freehling, "The Founding Fathers and Slavery," *American Historical Review* 77 (February 1972); Don B. Kates, "Abolition, Deportation, Integration: Attitudes toward Slavery in the Early Republic," *Journal of Negro History* 53 (January 1968).

SLAVERY AND PERSONALITY

American literature, Southern in particular, contains a multitude of Uncle Toms or Sambos who shuffle through the story lines of abolitionists and proslavery defenders. To some historians, the Uncle Tom was an abused and exploited faithful servant; but to others, he was an individual whose heart seethed with discontent while he acted out the expected part. For the latter group of Northern historians—Kenneth Stampp and Herbert Aptheker—"Sambo" for the most part did not exist. Stanley Elkins in *Slavery: A Problem in American Institutional and Intellectual Life* (Chicago: 1959) revived the plantation "Sambo" not as an example of slavery's beneficence, or Negro inferiority, but as a product of the dehumanization, infantilization, and personality-distorting powers of a totally closed institution. The debate on slavery's effects upon the personality is a relatively new one. The literature is sparse, but see Part III for the chief examples. The controversy provoked by Elkins's thesis on slave personality and Latin American bondage is discussed in Ann J. Lane, ed., *The Debate over Slavery: Stanley Elkins and His Critics* (Urbana, Ill.: 1971). The latest comprehensive treatment of this aspect is Eugene D. Genovese's *Roll, Jordan, Roll: The World the Slaves Made* (New York: 1974).

Afro-American folklore and slave songs are primary sources which must be consulted before any definitive conclusions can be reached on the question of the slave personality. Interesting collections of slave songs are James Weldon Johnson, *The Book of American Negro Spirituals* (New York: 1925) and his *The Second Book of Negro Spirituals* (New York: 1926); Natalie Curtis Burlin, *Negro Folk-Songs* Vols. I–IV (New York: 1918–1919); W. F. Allen, C. P. Ware, and L. McKim Garrison, *Slave Songs of the United States* (New York: 1867); W. E. Barton, *Old Plantation Hymns* (Boston: 1899). Studies have been made on these songs: Miles Mark Fisher's speculative but fascinating *Negro Slave Songs in the United States* (Ithaca, N.Y.: 1953); Sterling Brown, "Negro Folk

Expression," *Phylon* 14 (Spring 1953); Lawrence Levine's "Slave Songs and Slave Consciousness" disputes Elkins's Sambo thesis in Tomara K. Hareven, ed., *Anonymous Americans* (Englewood Cliffs, N.J.: 1971); also, Langston Hughes and Arna Bontemps, eds., *The Book of Negro Folklore* (New York: 1958) is a first-rate introduction into black folklore.

SLAVE RESISTANCE

The question of slave resistance is related to the debate over the slave personality and nature of slavery. If the level or amount of resistance is high, then it would appear that Sambo personality types do not dominate the plantations nor benign paternalism characterize the "peculiar institution." The work of the Marxist historian Herbert Aptheker began the attack upon the slave docility school, in *American Negro Slave Revolts* (New York: 1943). Informative general studies of slave resistance are: Joseph C. Carroll, *Slave Insurrections in the United States, 1800–1865* (Boston: 1938); Harvey Wish, "American Slave Insurrections Before 1861," *Journal of Negro History* 22 (July 1937); Nicholas Halasz, *The Rattling of Chains: Slave Unrest and Revolt in the Antebellum South* (New York: 1966). Inquiries into colonial slave resistance are found in Kenneth Scott, "The Slave Insurrection in New York in 1712," *N. Y. Historical Society Quarterly* 65 (January 1961); Ferenc Szasz, "The New York Slave Revolt of 1741: A Re-examination," *New York History* 48 (June 1967); and Gerald W. Mullin's *Flight and Rebellion: Slave Resistance in Eighteenth Century Virginia* (New York: 1972), the most recent word on the Gabriel Prosser rebellion which employs a sociological framework for analysis.

Two most important nineteenth-century slave insurrections, led by Denmark Vesey in 1822 and Nat Turner in 1831, have caused much comment: John Lofton, *Insurrection in South Carolina: The Turbulent World of Denmark Vesey* (Yellow Springs, Ohio: 1964) and Richard Wade, whose study doubts the existence of a plot, "The Vesey Plot Reconsidered," *Journal of Southern History* 30 (May 1964); F. Roy Johnson, *The Nat Turner Slave Insurrection* (Murfreesboro, N.C.: 1966). William Styron's novel, *The Confessions of Nat Turner* (New York: 1967) created a literary and historiographical controversy and antagonized many black intellectuals as evidenced in *William Styron's Nat Turner: Ten Black Writers Respond* edited by John Henrik Clarke (Boston: 1968). The debate is covered by John B. Duff and Peter M. Mitchell, eds., in *The Nat Turner Rebellion: The Historical Event and the Modern Controversy* (New York: 1971). Resistance did not always take the form of insurrections, as evidenced in Raymond and Alice Bauer's "Day to Day Resistance to Slavery," *Journal of Negro History*, 27 (October 1943); Larry Gara's *The Liberty Line* (Lexington, Ky.: 1961), which analyzes the myth and the reality behind the underground railroad; and Kenneth Stampp's *The Peculiar Institution* (New York: 1956), the best general study of American slavery.

PROFITABILITY, EXPANSION, AND POLITICS

The literature on the profitability of slavery is large and controversial. Charles Sydnor's conclusions in *Slavery in Mississippi* (Baton Rouge, La.: 1933) about the unprofitability of the institution in Mississippi are, on the whole, supported by Ralph B. Flanders, *Plantation Slavery in Georgia* (Chapel Hill, N.C.: 1933); and Charles S. Davis, *The Cotton Kingdom in Alabama* (Montgomery, Ala.: 1939). According to Harold D. Woodman's historiographical essay, "The Profitability of Slavery: A Historical Perennial," *Journal of Southern History* 29 (August 1963), these monographs and the immense influence of Phillips, who also held slavery to be unprofitable, dominated academic thinking on the subject until the appearance of important revisionist work by Robert R. Russel and Thomas Govan. In "The General Effects of Slavery Upon Southern Economic Progress," *Journal of Southern History* 4 (February 1938), Russel attributed the South's economic backwardness not to slavery, but to factors of climate, topography, natural resources, and the character of the white population. Govan's "Was Plantation Slavery Profitable?" *Journal of Southern History* 8 (November 1942) makes a strong case for slavery as a highly profitable business enterprise. Two Harvard economists, Alfred H. Conrad and John R. Meyer, in "The Economics of Slavery in the Ante Bellum South," *Journal of Political Economy* 66 (April 1958), conclude that slavery was profitable and did not hamper Southern economic growth. In the same issue of the *Journal of Political Economy*, Douglass F. Dowd registers his objections to the Conrad and Meyer thesis in a reply, "The Economics of Slavery in the Ante Bellum South: A Comment." Robert William Fogel and Stanley L. Engerman have written a widely acclaimed and controversial study, *Time on the Cross* 2 vols. (Boston: 1974), employing econometric and quantitative methodologies to prove slavery was a profitable and rather benign institution. Their work is the most recent general analysis of antebellum bondage.

The debate over the profitableness of slavery relates to its expansion into the western territories and concomitantly to the larger question of the necessity of a civil war to prevent that expansion. That slavery had reached its natural limits is a theory developed by Avery O. Craven, *Soil Exhaustion as a Factor in the Agricultural History of Virginia and Maryland* (Urbana, Ill.: 1926). Robert S. Starobin's *Industrial Slavery in the Old South* (New York: 1970) demonstrates that the commitment to slave industry in the South and its future use in the territories was a part of the growth of Southern nationalism. Northern and western opposition to the extension of slavery into the territories has been attributed to abolitionist, humanitarian, and racial egalitarian ideals. More recent studies have detected racism as a major component in antislavery extension sentiment: Eugene H. Berwanger, *The Frontier Against Slavery* (Urbana, Ill.: 1967) and George M. Fredrickson, *The Black Image in the White Mind* (New York: 1971). In Eric Foner's *Free Soil, Free Labor, Free Men: The Ideology of the Republican Party before the Civil War* (New York: 1970), racism, racial egalitarianism, and the belief in free western soil as a safety valve for Northern society perpetuating social mobility coalesce to form opposition to slavery expansion.

LATIN AMERICAN AND CARIBBEAN SLAVERY

The literature on slavery in the Western hemisphere is rapidly increasing. Frank Tannenbaum's *Slave and Citizen: The Negro in the Americas* (New York: 1947) and Stanley Elkins's *Slavery* (Chicago: 1959) began the debate and initiated the comparative study of slavery among American scholars. Many of the more recent studies challenge the Tannenbaum-Elkins view that Latin American slavery differed substantially from the institution as it operated in the American South: Marvin Harris, *Patterns of Race in the Americas* (New York: 1964); David Brion Davis, *The Problem of Slavery in Western Culture* (Ithaca, N.Y.: 1966); Carl Degler, *Neither Black nor White* (New York: 1970); and Pierre L. van den Berghe, *Race and Racism: A Comparative Perspective* (New York: 1967). Herbert Klein's *Slavery in the Americas: A Comparative Study of Virginia and Cuba* (Chicago: 1967) supports the Tannenbaum-Elkins view.

Brazilian slavery was the most significant in Latin America because of its large slave population and its influence on Brazilian culture and society. The classic studies are Gilberto Freye's *The Masters and the Slaves* (New York: 1946); Donald Pierson, *Negroes in Brazil* (Chicago: 1942); Arthur Ramos, *The Negro in Brazil* (Washington, D.C.: 1945). These studies are quite favorable to Brazilian slavery and race relations compared to the United States. Several of the newer studies are not so favorable to the Brazilian system: C. R. Boxer, *The Golden Age of Brazil 1695–1750* (Berkeley, Calif.: 1964); Carl N. Degler, "Slavery in Brazil and the United States," *American Historical Review* 65 (April 1970); and Florestan Fernandes, *The Negro in Brazilian Society* (New York: 1969). For an example of Brazilian slave resistance R. K. Kent's "Palmares: An African State in Brazil," *Journal of African History* 6 (1965) is an excellent study.

Slavery in Cuba and the West Indies has been studied less than in Brazil, nevertheless several first-rate studies exist. On Cuba the work of Herbert Klein, *Slavery in the Americas* (Chicago: 1967) and Ramiro Guerra y Sanchez, *Sugar and Society in the Caribbean* (New Haven, Conn.: 1964) are invaluable. Scholarly works on the British Caribbean are more abundant: Eric Williams's classic Marxist study analyzing the role of slavery in establishing British industrial capitalism, *Capitalism and Slavery* (Chapel Hill, N.C.: 1944); Philip Curtin, *Two Jamaicas* (Cambridge, England: 1955); Elsa V. Goveia, *Slave Society in the British Leeward Islands at the End of the 18th Century* (New Haven, Conn.: 1965); Bryan Edwards's wealth of information, *The Civil and Commercial History of the British Colonies in the West Indies*, 5 vols. (Philadelphia: 1793). Winthrop D. Jordan, "American Chiaroscuro: The Status and Definition of Mulattoes in the British Colonies," *William and Mary Quarterly* 19 (April 1962); Sidney Mintz, "Labor and Sugar in Puerto Rico and in Jamaica," *Comparative Studies* 1 (March 1959); Orlando Patterson's invaluable interdisciplinary study of Jamaica, *The Sociology of Slavery* (London: 1967); C. L. R. James, *The Black Jacobins*, 2d ed., (New York: 1963) is an exciting description and analysis of the Haitian slave revolt by a prominent black socialist. Gwendolyn M. Hall compares slave management in *Social Control in Slave Plantation Societies* (Baltimore: 1971).